Listen to the Crying of the Earth

Listen to the Crying of the Earth

Cultivating Creation Communities

Alvin Pitcher

THE PILGRIM PRESS
CLEVELAND, OHIO

The Pilgrim Press, Cleveland, Ohio 44115
© 1993 by William Alvin Pitcher

Biblical quotations are from the New Revised Standard Version of the Bible,
© 1989 by the Division of Christian Education of the National Council
of Churches of Christ in the U.S.A., and are used by permission

Printed in the United States of America
The paper used in this publication is acid free and meets the minimum
requirements of American National Standard for Information Sciences-Permanence
of Paper for Printed Library Materials, ANSI Z39.48-1984

98 97 96 95 94 93   5 4 3 2 1

Library of Congress Cataloging-in-Publication Data

Pitcher, W. Alvin.
Listen to the crying of the earth : cultivating creation communities / Alvin Pitcher.
        p.   cm.
Includes bibliographical references and index.
ISBN 0-8298-0961-9
1. Human ecology—Religious aspects—Christianity.
2. Environmental protection—Citizen participation.
I. Title. BT695.5.P57   1993
261.8'362—dc20   93-15430 CIP

Printed on recycled paper

Contents

Preface
Listening to and Caring for the Creation

Early in September 1989, I arrived at Holden Village, a church retreat center in the Cascade Mountains in the state of Washington, located on the site of an old Copper mine. A copy of *State of the World, 1987* was more or less by chance in a box of books I brought along for a nine-month sabbatical.

The nine months turned into twenty-one months, during which I listened to what the authors of that book were saying about how we were destroying our nonhuman life-support systems. While I focused on the crying of the earth, I also tried to understand why we had arrived at what seemed to me to be a disastrous state of affairs. In addition, I explored resources for moving in different directions, especially resources in the Christian tradition. Since that time, I have been especially concerned to develop some resources that can be used by churches in responding to the situation. This book represents my personal journey, oriented toward making up my mind about what the issues are and what might be done about them by ordinary lay church members and ordinary citizens. While this book is heavily influenced by my own Christian convictions and my own opinions about economic and political theory and practice, it is meant to address a broad spectrum of persons, some of whom inevitably will not share all of these convictions.

At the broadest level, we can say that the relationship between humans and the environment—the relationship between economic growth and the earth's needs—has been a perennial problem. However, the debate about how we are going to organize society to continue a path of economic growth is no longer what matters most. What matters is not the form of the social organization but the substance of the society, the goals and purposes of people and institutions. Broadly speaking, three different interpretations of the situation exist.

In one interpretation, that of the economic and military establishments and their supporting casts in the government and the universities, the situation does not especially need attention. Things are not as bad as the pessimists describe them, and even if they were, say the advocates of this position, there is not much that we can do about them. The kinds of actions environmentalists suggest would disrupt the present system and would require a call to action that is not present in the U.S. electorate. So, since we cannot do anything to *prevent,* for example, global warming, the best that we can do is to prepare to *respond* to it. This position is rooted in the self-interests of the dominant economic and military bureaucracies, but pointing this out does not help change the minds of such persons. There is no recognition in this view that the goals and purposes of the dominant institutions are being challenged by the present situation.

Another interpretation accepts the seriousness of our present situation in a more pessimistic stance and outlines responses based on the conviction that we can have our cake and eat it too. That is, supporters of this position propose technological innovations that will allow us to maintain the goal of economic growth while protecting the environment; they support the basic economic ideology behind the development of world markets. It is claimed, for example, that energy efficiency, supported by the government and by the persistent advocacy of its economic and thus market advantages, will allow us to produce as much if not more with much less damage to the environment. In this view, intelligent changes in the way we produce whatever we produce will meet the threats to the environment.

A third interpretation challenges the fundamental values of the Western industrial system. The goal of this social system and of its members, say those who challenge it, is to increase the production of goods and services, and—whether or not it is intentionally part of the system—the result is to increase the power, possessions, and prestige of the producers. The effects of such activity on the natural environment, on communities, on family life, and on the health and lifestyle of individuals are secondary and irrelevant. Everything is driven by the goal of increasing the amount of consumption, production, and profit.

Underlying this goal is the notion that the human being belongs to no larger meaningful reality except that which is useful to increase profits. To be truthful, the Western industrial system does foster some concern for the family and for the national interest, at least as far as such concern can improve the bottom line. Increasingly, however, there is no way to establish oneself in the context of a community and a way of life that is not subject to destruction. The absorption of family farms into agribusiness is an illustration of this—generations of history, of meaningful existence, are undermined overnight in the name of increased business efficiency.

Those who challenge the Western industrial system argue for and seek to organize institutions that support a different way of being. We do, say advocates of this position, belong to each other, to the natural world, and to the realities underlying it. In short, we belong to the ground of being, a higher power, to being itself: to God.

This book is organized, somewhat artificially, into four chapters. Chapter 1 is about listening to what the natural world (the creation) is saying to us. What is happening? What are the effects of global warming, ozone depletion, water pollution, waste disposal, Third World economics, population explosion, and the loss of soil, croplands, forests, species, clean air, and minerals? Chapter 2 relates these issues to social theory and practice: to economics, education, and politics. Chapter 3 shows how the Bible, liberation theology, process theology, and the theology of stewardship are related to environmental issues. Chapter 4 discusses how we can become a part of creation communities and respond to environmental problems through our churches, work, communities, politics, economic activity, and personal decisions. In the conclusion, we will explore how all of this is integrated into an understanding of our calling as human beings.

I come away from this study firmly convinced that the Word of God cannot be heard unless we listen to what God is saying through the creation, through environmental degradation, and through the current environmental revolution. The reason for the extensive material in chapter 1 on what is happening to the creation is the conviction that one must listen to that material over and over again if the Word of God is to be heard. There is no shortcut. The Bible alone is not enough, crucial though it may be. Theological discussion is not enough. Experiences in the wildernesses are not enough.

A second conviction is that the social institutions of our culture—economic, political, and educational—are inadequate in the way they understand and deal with the challenge.

A third conviction is that the Christian witness, insofar as it is organized around an image of God that is possessed by an individual and realized by an individual alone, will not provide a way out. There is no individual fulfillment. We are fulfilled and sanctified only in relation to each other, the natural world, and God.

It is clear to me that we are in the beginning of another Reformation. No one knows where it will go. It is out of our hands. At the same time, we are called to discern the signs of the times and search for the content of our calling.

Holden Village has been the setting, the occasion, and the encouragement for this undertaking. I am indebted to Scott Haasarud, the director of Holden Village, who has put many resources at my disposal; to Roger Strom for technical assistance with the computer and for his quiet, helpful presence; to Teak Kilmer for editorial assistance; to Richard Brown of Pilgrim Press for his encouragement and detailed suggestions; to Bob Olander for copyediting; and to Sara and Paul for graciously supporting my focus on the project. In addition, the support and nourishment of dozens of special persons in University Church in Chicago, the Covenantal Community of University Church in Chicago, the environmental student groups at the University of Chicago, and the Holden Community family have been vital to this effort.

1

What Is Happening to the Earth?
The Ecological Crisis

Almost without our being aware of it, human activity has affected the physical, chemical, and biological framework of human life—what we refer to as nature, the natural world, the nonhuman reality, or the earth. For example, changes in the capacity of the atmosphere to allow heat radiation to escape the earth, allegedly produced by increases in the "greenhouse" gases (carbon dioxide, chlorofluorocarbons, methane, nitrous oxide), threaten to raise the earth's temperature, with resulting changes in rainfall, growing seasons, the location of forests and croplands, and the level of the oceans.

Increasing amounts of certain gases, especially chlorofluorocarbons, reduce the amount of ozone in the stratosphere, which results in more ultraviolet rays reaching the earth's surface. Many believe that this will cause increased skin cancer, weaken the immune system, lead to blindness for unprotected eyes. Plant growth may also be affected negatively.

The increased use of water, especially for irrigation, is creating water shortages and threatening the availability of water in the future. Water tables are going down. The water in aquifers (strata of soil, rock, and sand in which water is stored) is being depleted. The struggle between Israel and the Palestinians over the water resources of the Jordan River basin is an example of the crucial nature of the issue. The rise in ocean levels will eventually threaten the water sources for cities with intakes at the mouths of rivers, as the salt water flows farther upstream. Pollution threatens water quality. The increasing amounts of garbage as well as industrial and military wastes often meet the increasing resistance of communities to accept waste disposal facilities. Because experts cannot agree on an acceptable way to dispose of nuclear waste, such waste continues to stockpile. The presence of other less toxic wastes constitutes a major problem. Billions, some say trillions, of dollars will be required to clean up toxic waste sites, especially if we include the toxic wastes from military establishments.

The world population, now a little over 5 billion, is expected to reach 8.6 billion by 2025 and 10 billion by 2040. Ninety-five percent of the increase will be in the developing nations, in which the resources to support even the present population are frequently lacking. The result will be famine, overuse of land, deforestation, soil erosion, and a further gap between the haves and the have-nots. The social and political conflicts both internally and externally will increase. For example, some predict that Mexico's population will double before it levels off, putting further pressure on the southern border of the United States.

Each year an estimated fifteen million acres of land are degraded beyond hope of reclamation. About fifty million more acres become unprofitable to farm or graze. About 35 percent of the total cultivatable land is threatened with becoming desert. Deforestation, drought, overgrazing, poor drainage on irrigated land—all contribute to the degradation of land.

The surge in food production with the green revolution is now slowing down, and we are threatened by the polluting effects of fertilizers and pesticides. Production and consumption per capita are actually declining in Africa. There are at present an estimated 1.2 billion persons worldwide chronically hungry, without adequate shelter and clothing. Estimates of 40,000 children aged five and under dying every day of hunger and hunger-related diseases point to the scope of the problem.

Deforestation, population explosion, ozone depletion, global warming, land degradation, species depletion—all of these problems involve the practices and policies of developed nations both internally and in relation to developing nations. Some claim, for instance, that population control will never take place without economic and social development in developing nations. Development that is the basis for a change in the status, roles, and economic opportunities of women especially is important. The developed countries must aid developing countries with huge infusions of capital, debt forgiveness, and changes in social policy to provide alternatives to ozone-depleting chemicals, technologies that substitute for fossil fuel energy, alternatives to forest destruction, and substitutes for harmful pesticides, the toxic residues of which are found in the food we and others import. Pressure in governments in developing nations to change land ownership policies is very important.

By-products of the use of coal, oil, and natural gas are responsible for what is called acid rain. The acids affect the health of trees and thus of their resistance to pests and diseases. Over 35 percent of Europe's forests, by some estimates, have been affected.

The destruction of tropical rain forests, especially to establish live-stock ranches and plots for impoverished peasants, is responsible for the disappearance of a significant number of species—the loss is estimated at between four and six thousand species per year. Thus the world's genetic pool, developed over billions of years, is being depleted. No one knows ex-actly how important that pool is; humanity has used about 7,500 of the 75,000 species known to have edible parts. The importance of this genetic pool in light of genetic engineering is also difficult to assess.

Our industrial society produces sulfur oxides, nitrogen oxides, hydro-carbons, carbon monoxide, particulates, and lead, all of which are health hazards. Ozone, so beneficial in the stratosphere, is a hazard at low alti-tudes. These substances are responsible in part for certain cancers, genetic defects, respiratory diseases, and heart problems.

Finally, resources crucial to our industrial society—at least as it func-tions at present—are being used up at rates that threaten their availability for future generations. Reserves of petroleum, if present use patterns con-tinue, will last another eighty-five years, according to some estimates.

Other estimates are more optimistic, still others, more pessimistic. Yet the fundamental issue is much more important than the accuracy of such estimates. The issue is, what kind of development is possible for the developing nations, where most of the people of the world are and will be living? What chance of survival does our present lifestyle have if everyone adopts it? Is not the future with those who can find a way of living without the abuse of current resources, many of which are in limited supply?

In sum, threats to our life-support systems are sending a message to those with eyes to see and ears to hear. If we pay attention to the results of our way of life, it is clear that something fundamental is wrong. Listening to what scientists and students of the environment are telling us about our life-support systems is an essential part of assessing our current situation. Some persons find this listening so disheartening and so threatening to their present structure of meaning that they enter a stage of denial. Yet it is essential to attend in some detail to what is going on if one wants to hear the Word of God in our times.

There may be no way to convince the skeptics who insist that there really is no ozone problem or global warming problem, or that humans are not responsible for these problems. Nevertheless, the following sections will discuss these and other issues in some detail. If the portrayal of these problems seems too overwhelming, I suggest that you turn first to Chapter 3 for perspectives on action or to Chapter 4 for some practical suggestions on participating in the environmental revolution in a constructive, meaningful way.

Global Warming

Although there is little agreement about the exact effects of global warming, for many persons the most threatening environmental issue today is the possibility of climate change due to global warming. In the video "After the Warming," for example, James Burke traces the relation between climate change and the rise and fall of civilizations.

In brief, here is how global warming is thought to occur: certain gases produced by our industrial and life processes rise to the stratosphere, from ten to twenty-five miles up, to form a blanket around the earth. These gases let sunlight in and prevent certain heat radiations from escaping into space. The more these gases accumulate in the stratosphere, the more heat is contained and the warmer the atmosphere becomes. The chief gases involved are carbon dioxide (57 percent), chlorofluorocarbons (25 percent), methane (12 percent), and nitrous oxide (6 percent).[1] The percentages represent estimates of the responsibility for warming assigned to each gas. Carbon dioxide stays in the atmosphere several years, nitrous oxide and chlorofluorocarbons from 75 to 150 years, methane about 11 years. The predicted rise in the daily average temperature of the atmosphere, from 1 to 3 degrees centigrade by the year 2030 or sometime shortly thereafter, allegedly is due to the doubling of the amount of warming gases from preindustrial times. While almost everyone couches their predictions in tentative terms and suggests numerous qualifications, such as the uncertainty about the role of cloud formations, most experts expect significant warming. Such warming will likely result in the melting of the polar icecaps, which, together with the expansion of water in the oceans, will cause a significant rise in ocean levels. Disastrous floods in the delta areas of the Ganges and the Nile are expected. In anticipation, Holland has spent billions of dollars to raise the height of its dikes.

The most convincing evidence is the studies that chart the correlation between the amount of carbon dioxide in the atmosphere and the average daily temperature for the last 160,000 years. Ice cores from the

Greenland glaciers have been found to contain bubbles of air thousands of years old. The carbon dioxide content of these bubbles is correlated with other particles in the ice cores and with sediments discovered in lake bottoms to determine both the temperature and the amount of carbon dioxide in the air.

Chlorofluorcarbons, responsible for 25 percent of the warming effects, are also a major cause of ozone depletion and will be discussed in the next section. Carbon dioxide, responsible for roughly 57 percent of the warming effects, is the result of the burning of fossil fuels (44 percent) and the decay and burning of forests and other vegetation (13 percent). The use of fossil fuels produced 5.66 billion tons of carbon in 1988, and the amount produced by the burning of forests is variously estimated at between 1 and 2.6 billion tons of carbon.[2]

Clearly, we have only indirect control over the burning of tropical forests through such measures as the World Bank's policy in loaning money to developing nations, negotiations regarding debt forgiveness, programs to exchange technology, and compensation in exchange for the control of forest cutting. We do, however, have some chance to change the situation in the areas of our own power generation, our use of electricity, and our use of gasoline and natural gas.

The United States, which makes up 4.61 percent of the world's population, is responsible for more than one-quarter of world emissions of carbon dioxide. If all peoples used fossil fuels at the rate we do, carbon emissions would be over thirty billion tons per year—an amount impossible to sustain from the point of view of fossil fuel resources and unthinkable from the viewpoint of global warming.

Researchers have suggested that carbon emissions be cut to about 2 billion tons per year worldwide. This clearly puts a heavy responsibility on the United States. How do we move in this direction?

The proposal that natural gas be substituted for oil, which produces 44 percent more carbon, and for coal, which produces 75 percent more carbon, is rejected by Christopher Flavin (see *Worldwatch Paper 91*) because methane leaks in the distribution of natural gas offset the benefits (methane being one of the gases with greenhouse effects). Furthermore, while there is considerable natural gas worldwide, the U.S., in relative terms, does not have much.

The proposal to scrub emissions from power plants and industrial plants is countered by the problem of cost—electricity rates would rise by one-third—and the problem of waste disposal from scrubbing. Burial in the ocean is currently the only proposed disposal method.

Many advocate increasing energy efficiency as both effective in reducing carbon emissions and as cost-effective; a resource in limited supply would be saved, and the threat from carbon dioxide would be reduced. Some claim that electrical motors could be 40 percent more efficient, refrigerators could be 25 percent more efficient, and lighting—responsible for 17 percent of fossil fuel use—could be 80 percent more efficient with the use of fluorescent lights.[3] Cogeneration, using a combination of heat and electricity generation, could save from 24 to 40 percent. In transportation, responsible for 10 percent of carbon emissions (550 million tons), some predicted that carbon emissions will rise 75 percent by 2010 unless drastic changes occur. There is little question that relatively safe cars could be produced to get fifty miles per gallon and that, relatively soon, sixty or seventy miles per gallon is not unreasonable to expect. Prototypes already exist. The expansion of mass transportation facilities, such as those proposed for Los Angeles, are part of a rational program for the future. If energy efficiency increases at the rate of 3 percent per year, fossil fuel emissions of carbon will still be 6 million tons per year. That seems too great a risk to take. Proposals for increasing the use of nuclear power are surfacing with renewed energy. According to Christopher Flavin, increasing costs, the continued danger of accidents, and the lack of acceptable procedures for the storing of wastes are sufficient to prevent much further development.

Replacing fossil fuel use with renewable sources of energy where possible is a necessity. All kinds of alternatives are being developed, albeit slowly: solar, wind, methane, solar photovoltaic, biomass, geothermal. To fund such research the European Community is considering an increase in gasoline taxes.

Standards for energy efficiency in homes and for appliances established in California in the 1970s have resulted in as much as 50 percent less energy used per person as compared to Texas, for example. Such standards could be developed nationally, and more money could be allocated to research for alternative energy sources and for energy-efficient technologies.

In addition, a program to encourage the planting of trees could be subsidized. According to Flavin, 1 hectare (2.478 acres) of trees, during a period of rapid growth, takes about 5 tons of carbon out of the atmosphere in temperate zones and 5.5 tons in tropical regions.[4] One power company is planting trees in Guatemala to offset the effect of carbon emissions from a new power plant. This could be a national policy in this and other countries. I was told by an employee of a logging company that in one redwood forest the U.S. government requires sixteen trees to be planted for every tree cut. Proposals to cut deforestation in half could eliminate as much as 830 tons of carbon emissions per year worldwide.

All of this simply indicates that aggressive leadership nationally and internationally could go a long way toward removing the threat of global warming. Recent events in connection with the 1992 Earth Summit in Rio de Janeiro certainly indicate that the United States is not committed to assume much of this leadership, although European nations and Japan seem prepared to move whether or not the United States does.

So, what are we hearing? We would be wise to reduce the use of fossil fuels and the burning of biomass, even if in the form of ethanol. (If all the U.S. corn crop were used to make ethanol, only 20 percent of our petroleum requirements would be met.) This reduction could be achieved by the efficient use of energy, by the development of renewable energy resources, and by a change in our lifestyle that would result in less use of energy.

Ozone Depletion

Having discussed the way in which our natural world is saying something to us through the phenomenon of global warming, I turn now to what the natural world is saying to us through ozone depletion. First I will summarize reports on the current depletion of the ozone layer and predictions about future depletion. Then I will report on the alleged causes of the depletion and its impact on human, animal, and plant life. Finally I will discuss proposals to prevent further depletion of the ozone and suggest what we can do about it.

Ozone, a gas in which each molecule contains three atoms of oxygen, is produced in the stratosphere by chemical reactions triggered by sunlight. It is also produced near the earth by lightning, by electric sparks from motors, and by sunlight acting on the nitrogen oxides from auto fumes. At the ground level, ozone is about one part per million parts of the atmosphere; in the stratosphere approximately seven to fifteen miles up, it is about six parts per million parts of the atmosphere. When present in the stratosphere, ozone prevents certain ultraviolet rays from reaching the earth, rays that damage human, animal, and plant life. Scientists hold that certain gases produced by human activity under certain conditions destroy ozone molecules.

Recent research has discovered that something is happening to the stratospheric ozone layer. Depletion is particularly evident in the Antarctic, where, in an area the size of the United States, ozone levels dropped by about 50 percent from August to October 1989. In some areas, ozone has been completely absent. This entire area is referred to as the ozone hole.[5] Studies indicate that south of latitude 60 degrees south, the ozone has been depleted by 5 percent since 1979. (Worldwide, the average concentration was down about 2 percent between 1969 and 1986.) Over Europe, North America, and the former Soviet Union, ozone is currently down 3 percent in the summer and 4.7 percent in the winter. While there is uncertainty about just how much the ozone layer is depleted, there seems to be agreement that it is occurring faster than most researchers predicted. UV-B, consisting of the ultraviolet rays within the 290 to 320 nanometer band, the most dangerous biologically, are predicted to rise between 5 and 20 percent during the next forty years in the most populated areas of the world.[6]

The Impact of More UV-B Radiation

The results of this ozone depletion, which affects the ozone layer's ability to filter out high frequency ultraviolet rays, are found in the statistics on skin cancer. Skin cancer is more prevalent today, and while some of this is attributed to more outdoor activity, researchers connect the increase with the depletion of the ozone and expect skin cancer rates to continue to rise. Thus it is predicted that for every 1 percent drop in ozone, squamous and basal cell carcinoma will increase by from 4 to 6 percent, and that from 3 to 15 million new cases of these types of cancer will occur in Americans born before 2075. The Environmental Protection Agency (EPA) estimates that from 31,000 to 126,000 cases of melanoma, a more deadly form of skin cancer, will occur among U.S. caucasians born before 2075. (It is worth noting that light-skinned people are more susceptible to these forms of cancer.) In Australia, death from melanoma is now five times more common than it was fifty years ago.[7] This is particularly significant because one would expect the effects of the Antarctic ozone hole to be noticeable there.

EPA studies also predict that from 550,000 to 2.8 million Americans born before 2075 will suffer from cataracts because of the increase of UV-B radiation.[8] Dire predictions are also made about the effect of ozone depletion on the immune system; some believe that it will lessen the effectiveness of inoculation programs. Researchers also claim that a good percentage of plant species, including many crops, will be negatively affected. Phytoplankton, the backbone of aquatic food, responded to a simulated 25-percent reduction of ozone with a loss of 35 percent of its growth. Zooplankton, the larva of some fish species, some shellfish, and anchovies—all indicate negative reactions to decreases in the ozone level.[9]

Increased ultraviolet rays also affect synthetic materials, such as polyvinyl chloride, with resulting damages estimated to be $4.7 billion by 2075.[10] Further, these rays lead to more ozone at ground level, thus increasing smog and threatening air quality. EPA studies indicate that potential losses in the U.S. from ozone destruction are in the range of $6 trillion through the year 2075.[11]

The Causes of Ozone Depletion

Ozone forms when ultraviolet rays from the sun dissociate the ordinary oxygen molecule (consisting of two atoms of oxygen) into two single atoms of oxygen. These single atoms may then combine with ordinary oxygen molecules to form ozone (which consists of three atoms of oxygen). Ozone molecules are broken up by chlorine or bromine to form chlorine or bromine monoxide and molecular oxygen. Then the C10 molecule reacts with another oxygen atom formed by the dissociation of ozone to form chlorine or bromine and molecular oxygen. The same chlorine or bromine is then ready to begin the process all over again. Thus a single atom of chlorine or bromine can act over and over again to destroy ozone molecules. Two other gases also destroy ozone: carbon tetrachloride and methyl chloroform.

Chlorine and bromine are released into the atmosphere by the chlorofluorocarbons and halons used in industrial processes. CFC-11, CFC-12, and CFC-113 provide chlorine. Halon-1301 and Halon-1211 provide bromine. CFC-11, responsible for 26 percent of the ozone depletion in the stratosphere, is used in blowing foams, aerosols, and refrigeration. CFC-12, responsible for 45 percent of the ozone depletion, is used in blowing foams, refrigeration, aerosols, and air conditioning. CFC-113, responsible for 12 percent of the ozone depletion, is used as a solvent, primarily to clean computer chips. Halon-1301, responsible for 4 percent of the ozone depletion, is used in fire extinguishers. Halon-1211, responsible for 1 percent of the ozone depletion, is also used in fire extinguishers. Carbon tetrachloride, responsible for 8 percent of the ozone depletion, is used as a solvent, as is methyl chloroform, responsible for 5 percent of the ozone depletion.[12]

Chlorofluorocarbons in the stratosphere also create the greenhouse effect. They are said to be responsible for 15 to 20 percent of the warming trend.[13] Chlorofluorocarbons have a life expectancy of 76 to 139 years in the stratosphere.[14] One molecule of CFC-12 traps as much heat as fifteen thousand molecules of carbon dioxide.[15]

Some governments have taken steps to reduce the use of the culprit gases. At Montreal in September 1987, twenty-four nations agreed to a program to freeze CFC production at 1986 levels by 1989, to achieve a 20 percent reduction by 1993, and to reach another 30 percent reduction by 1998. Halon production was to be frozen at 1986 levels beginning in 1992. How this was to be done was left to the individual nations.[16]

This agreement will slow the acceleration of the depletion, but it will not stop it. Gases already released, which take from seven to eight years to reach the stratosphere, are still on their way. Loopholes permit the former Soviet Union and the East European countries to meet their current five-year plans as long as use of CFCs and halons does not exceed .6 kilograms per capita per year. Developing countries have a ten-year grace period, during which growth up to .3 kilograms per capita for domestic needs is acceptable; they must freeze and then cut consumption by 50 percent.[17] Even with total support for the protocol, many predict that by 2075 the amount of chlorine in the stratosphere will triple.[18] Forty-five percent of the chlorine growth is said to be from exceptions to the ban, and 40 percent from chemicals not covered: carbon tetrachloride and methyl chloroform.[19] Technically, it is possible to reduce CFCs and halons by 90 percent by 1995. Sweden has acted to virtually eliminate production by 1995.[20]

Various countries have instituted programs to prevent the culprit gases already produced from reaching the stratosphere. These programs include the collection of coolants from old refrigerators; the collection and recycling of coolants from repaired or discarded air conditioners; the recovery of blowing foams; the incineration of foams; the recovery of the solvent CFC-113; new design, operating, and maintenance standards for refrigeration and air conditioning equipment; and designs that eliminate the need for harmful products.

Such innovative programs show that chlorine and bromine gases could be eliminated with further action by governments and by industries—actions to prohibit the manufacture of harmful gases, to support research that provides alternatives, and to reduce the effects of the gases already in use or scheduled for use.

Water Quantity and Quality

The survival of the human species, and of many others, is at stake if the management of the earth's water resources is not given immediate attention.

The World Resources Institute estimates that of the 41,000 cubic kilometers of water that are transferred from the oceans to the atmosphere and then returned to the earth in the form of precipitation, about 9,000 cubic kilometers are available to human use. This is enough, says the institute, to support twenty billion persons. The availability of water varies in different countries, and at present the amount used per capita varies widely. The average American, for example, consumes about seventy times as much as the average Ghanian. About 73 percent of the water available is used in irrigation, and about 37 percent of this irrigation water is used by plants.[21] Thus the allocation of the rights to use water is a major problem, since many rivers and lakes are shared not only by several states and regions but also, in some instances, by several countries.

The use of water for one purpose in one location drastically affects what is available in other areas. For example, using water for irrigation from the rivers flowing into the Aral Sea has caused the sea's water level to fall, leaving salt deposits exposed. This salt is then blown by the wind and falls on agricultural land, making it less fertile. The sea's water level continues to drop; the old shoreline is now about fifty kilometers from the water.

Supplies of water can be increased by mining underground water, by damming rivers, and by desalinizing ocean water. Increasing deforestation affects the runoff rates of water and makes the holding of water by dams more important than ever. Some researchers predict that global warming will increase precipitation from 7 to 15 percent, and many believe that the distribution of precipitation will also change. Thus, dam capacities in river basins will be more and more important. Groundwaters are being used up, especially in China, India, and the United States. In 1983, experts estimated that of the twenty-six billion cubic meters of mined groundwater, one-fifth was not replaceable.

The misuse of water for irrigation where proper drainage has not been installed causes water tables to remain high, resulting in the drowning of seedlings and plants. Excessive irrigation also results in excessive amounts of salt remaining in the soil. The leveling of the land can decrease the amount of water used by as much as 90 percent. Waterlogging is also prevented by such procedures. A sprinkler system can increase efficiency to as high as 70 percent, a great improvement over the gravity system in which water flows in furrows. Drop tubes can be attached to sprinkler systems, which when used in conjunction with special land preparation methods, can result in as much as 98 percent efficiency. Energy requirements also drop 20 to 30 percent. Microirrigation has been introduced for fruits, vegetables, and orchard crops. Drip, or trickle, irrigation, as this method is called, involves porous pipes on or below the soil surface. In addition, devices are available to measure the water needs of the soil so that irrigation occurs only when it is needed.[22]

Cropland procedures that allow for fallow years and for leaving crop residues on the field to absorb moisture from harvest to planting time eleven months later can vastly increase yields.[23]

The recycling and reuse of water in U.S. industry and cities can also greatly reduce the demand of water. In industry, reuse rates have climbed from 1.82 percent in all manufacturing in 1954 to 3.4 percent in 1978 and an estimated 8.6 percent in 1986. This rate could reach 17.08 percent by 2000. If this level is reached, water use, taking into account economic growth, will be about 45 percent lower than in 1978, when manufacturing used 49 billion cubic meters of water. In some places in the former Soviet Union, oil refineries are reusing water in such a fashion that no wastewater is discharged. Strict pollution control requirements can lead to water reuse, the recovery of valuable materials, the saving of money, and less pollution. Sweden and Israel are examples of nations with strict controls that have resulted in increased outputs—as much as three times—per unit of water used.[24]

Municipalities have techniques available to treat sewage by removing solids and organic matter by biological methods as well as further upgrading by chemical methods. The level of treatment depends on the standards required by governmental agencies. Policymakers have it within their power to reduce greatly the demand for new water. The potential exists for the collection of nutrients from water, nutrients that could replace the artificial fertilizers now used. One calculation suggests that it would take fifty-three million barrels of oil to provide the fertilizer equivalent of the nutrients in wastewaters produced in the United States in one year.[25]

Urban water requirements represent about one-tenth of the water withdrawals worldwide. Conservation policies can cut water use. In Tucson, Arizona, several policies are in place: increases in water prices, educational programs about restricting outdoor use to alternating days and certain hours, and encouragement of the use of water-saving devices for toilets, clothes washers, shower heads, and faucets. For example, conventional toilets using nineteen liters per flush can be replaced with common low-flow toilets using eleven liters, washdown types using four liters, or air-assisted models using two liters.

The *quality* of water is as important as its *quantity*. Increasingly, human activity is producing pollutants that find their way into our water supplies. The greatly increased use of fertilizers and pesticides threatens groundwater sources with unhealthy amounts of toxic materials. Similarly, the increasing seepage from waste dumps of all kinds threaten groundwater sources. The dumping of industrial and human wastes in rivers, lakes, and oceans continues in most parts of the world, making it difficult and costly to secure "pure" water.

Some researchers predict that global warming will cause the ocean levels to rise from two to six feet during the next century. This rise will cause ocean saltwater to push into river mouths and threaten the intake sources at the mouths of many rivers, including the Hudson in New York and the Delaware in Philadelphia.

The water crisis can be illustrated by what has been happening in El Salvador:

> Look at a body of water in El Salvador and you will see a reflection of almost every major environmental problem in the country: pesticide and fertilizer contamination; industrial pollution; municipal waste and sewage; sedimentation from deforestation and soil erosion; and waterborne diseases. All the major waterways in El Salvador are contaminated by raw sewage and a variety of toxic chemicals, according to a 1982 report by the U.S. Agency for International Development.
>
> Unburdened by governmental environmental regulations, a host of industries including textile factories, tanneries, slaughterhouses, and pesticide formulating plants freely dump their toxic wastes into waterways to cut costs and boost profits . . . Among the most notorious offenders are the more than 200 coffee processing plants . . . owned by the coffee oligarchy. These plants spew boron, chloride, and arsenic contaminated wastewater into rivers and streams throughout the country. The government . . . has extended sewage systems to only 15 percent of the countryside and 38 percent of the urban population, and only one in ten Salvadorans has access to safe drinking water. As a result gastrointestinal infections that could be prevented by cleaner water remain a leading cause of death throughout the country. . . .
>
> El Salvador's water is threatened by agriculture as well. Soil eroding from agricultural fields eventually flows as pesticide-laced sediment to the Pacific Ocean, where it is choking El Salvador's coastal mangroves to death. While once there were 296,000 acres of mangroves in the country, today sediments and deforestation have left only 6,888 acres. . . . As the mangroves disappear they take with them the shrimp and fish populations that breed in the shelter of their root systems.[26]

This illustrates the vast difficulties that exist in developing an adequate water supply in various parts of the world. One could duplicate this story in many countries, in both urban and rural areas.

Pollutants entering the atmosphere from industrial processes, especially nitrous oxide and sulfur dioxide, result in acid rain, which not only causes forests and other crops to die but also falls on lakes, causing them to become acidic and thus inhospitable to plant growth. In addition, organic wastes entering the disposal system and ending up in lakes causes the excessive growth of algae, which, when they decay, use up oxygen in the water. This process, eutrophication, negatively affects all marine life.

The pollution of lakes and rivers is reversible given resources and time. Groundwater is another matter. In her book *Earthright*, Patricia Hynes reports that "in their report, *Danger on Tap*, the National Wildlife Federation found that nearly half of the 201,000 public water systems in the United States violated the Safe Drinking Water Act during the fiscal year 1987" by exceeding pollution standards, failing to report violations, and failing to test for contaminants.[27] There are no functioning procedures to reverse this situation; many of the violations involved groundwater sources that cannot be cleaned.

The overall quality of water in coastal areas is deteriorating, with beaches being closed because of pathogenic bacteria and fish populations declining.

An article in *Arizona Trend* points to some of the ways in which water is an issue in one state.[28] In Arizona, enough water can be mined by drilling wells to serve any anticipated population for many, many years, although there is some uncertainty about the amount of pollution in the water. The issue then becomes how much water should be used in what time span. Neighboring New Mexico, it is said, will have pumped its wells dry in forty years at current rates. What then is the responsibility of this generation to future generations? The present law simply requires new developments to guarantee one hundred years of water. A new proposal seeks to limit water use in some new developments to a certain amount from the wells for each acre of land developed. Proponents of the law claim that there is nothing to stop anyone from purchasing water from other sources. Some assert that the Colorado River has plenty of water to provide whatever might be needed. Just how it is decided who should get the water from the Colorado, which flows into California and Mexico, is not clear. It is clear that some regional authority as well as a state authority is needed to allocate the available water. Furthermore, treatment plants for sewage already provide water for parks and golf courses, and there seems to be no limit other than cost to prevent much more use of treated water. With increasing standards for the discharge of sewage into rivers, the cost to consumers of treated water should decline.

Several messages are being conveyed by what heretofore we have considered a kind of free gift—namely, water. We cannot assume that there will always be water for drinking and cooking. The problem will only be compounded with the population explosion. In many parts of the world there is no way to guarantee water for the growing of crops. We shall see later how increasing areas of land are becoming deserts.

The political problems involved in the allocation of water and the protection of water from pollution are increasing, and they can only become more acute. Regional, national, and international agreements and the more stringent administration of water use are essential.

Waste Creation and Disposal

Having considered global warming, ozone depletion, and water resources, the fourth environmental issue is waste. Wastes from animals, industrial processes, and home operations are killing us as well as plant and animal life. Excessive wastes are burying us, creating conditions that threaten our health and use up the resources of the earth at an unnecessarily rapid rate.

We are poisoning ourselves, killing marine life, affecting plant growth, and contributing to ozone depletion. We are poisoning ourselves by using toxic materials to grow food, materials that threaten health and life as they pollute what we eat, what we drink, and what we breathe. We are poisoning ourselves by the irresponsible disposal of toxic materials in landfills and bodies of water. We are killing the animal life of the oceans and other bodies of water and the plants on which they feed by the irresponsible disposal of toxic wastes.

It takes much less energy to produce aluminum, steel, glass, and paper from recycled materials than it does from raw materials. Thus, by not recycling, we produce much more carbon dioxide—carbon dioxide that is responsible for global warming.

By not recycling our air conditioners and refrigerators, we allow the chemicals used in them to escape into the atmosphere, eventually rising up to help destroy the ozone layer.

Not only does it take more energy to produce goods from new materials, it also takes more water and uses up metals and trees, which eventually end up as wastes.

We are filling up space with garbage, space that, unless carefully monitored, will be unusable for other purposes. The Japanese have demonstrated how such space, when monitored, can be used for dual purposes.

We are creating difficult political situations and putting ourselves in an imperialistic posture as we and other industrial nations dump wastes in the developing nations of the world. The lack of international standards results in industries seeking places where wastes can be created and dumped without regard to the costs to people—and especially to future generations.

Responding to this situation, many environmentalists have proposed that we institute policies and practices that reduce the amount of material to be thrown away. Reusable containers have been mandated in some countries. The reduction of packaging is an obvious solution. Using personal cloth or string bags for groceries reduces waste, as does buying fewer products.

Environmentalists also propose that we recycle more of what is being thrown away: paper, glass, metal, tires, oil, appliances, plastics, batteries, yard wastes, and organic material; that we produce and use fewer materials that are not degradable; and that we bury less, incinerating everything possible. These proposals deserve attention.

Treating toxic wastes with special care when constructing and monitoring waste sites is also on the environmentalists' agenda.

Old waste sites can be opened up, recycling certain materials and establishing methane-collecting mechanisms (to produce energy) where feasible. Other efforts can encourage people to think about waste reduction, preferably rewarding it so that all industrial decisions are made with a view to reducing wastes.

The pesticides involved in agriculture not only contain contaminants that farm workers breathe but also contaminate the food produced as well as the soil and the water. Pesticide residues, allegedly cancer risks, have been found in cereals, eggs, vegetables, and other foods in India; in the breast milk of Indian mothers; in the breast milk of Nicaraguan mothers; in Latin American coffee beans; and in food produced in the United States. Tomatoes, beef, potatoes, oranges, and lettuce lead the list of contaminated foods. The National Resource Council estimates that pesticides in food will result in twenty thousand additional cancer patients per year. The residue of pesticides that have been banned in the United States are sometimes found in imported foods.

Groundwater has been contaminated with seventeen different pesticides in at least twenty-three states. Atrazine and alachlor, known to be a probable carcinogen, were the most frequently found. According to one estimate, fifty million persons are at risk from pesticide use in areas where groundwater is used for drinking.

Pesticides do not always control the pests they are designed to attack, particularly since many pests have developed resistance. Proven alternatives to chemicals exist. For example, an integrated pest management (IPM) program has been developed, combining the use of natural pest predators and crop planning patterns, the genetic development of pest-resistant crop varieties, and the judicious use of chemicals.

We are also poisoning ourselves with toxic wastes that are dumped into bodies of water—rivers, lakes, and oceans—and deposited in landfills without adequate guarantees that they will not leak into the soil. Indiscriminate, irresponsible industrial chemical waste and sewage disposal methods abound. Over 80,000 pits, ponds, and lagoons used for dumping wastes were discovered to be without liners to prevent seepage. The Superfund, created in 1986 to clean up these areas, is about $90 billion short of what is needed—some say $500 billion to $5 trillion short, if military wastes are included.

These toxic wastes also poison marine life, both plant and animal. In the process of poisoning fish, we poison ourselves.

It is clear that we do not have in place an adequate system to deal with toxic wastes. The public will suffer increased health problems unless a different approach is adopted both to clean up the present waste sites and to prevent the production of toxic wastes. The experience of other countries and of some plants in the United States indicates that much can be done to reduce the production of toxic wastes, much of it cost-effective.[29]

We discharge 160 million tons of garbage every year, about 3.5 pounds per person. Japan, by contrast, discards about 1.9 pounds per person, with roughly the same rate of income per capita as in the United States. Japan recycled 50 percent at its peak, in contrast to our 10 percent. The content of U.S. garbage is by weight about 41 percent paper, 18 percent yard wastes, 8.7 percent metals, 8.2 percent glass, 7.9 percent food, 6.5 percent plastics, 3.7 percent wood, and 1 percent toxic materials.[30] After one use, we discard two-thirds of aluminum, three-quarters of steel and paper, and an even higher percentage of plastics. We could recycle metal, glass, and a good part of the paper. Even some plastics are now being recycled.

Reusing aluminum saves 90 to 97 percent of the energy used in the production of aluminum from bauxite ore. Some 47 to 74 percent of the energy used in the production of new steel can be saved. Some 23 to 74 percent of the energy used in producing paper can be saved.[31] When energy is saved, less greenhouse-producing carbon dioxide and less acid rain-producing sulfur and nitrogen are released. Fewer trees are cut down, leaving more trees to use carbon dioxide and to prevent soil erosion. There are fewer wastes from the production process. All mining and logging wastes are eliminated, and less water is used.

Lawn wastes can be composted. Some municipalities have central locations to dispose of lawn wastes. Some have ordinances forbidding the collection of lawn wastes, forcing individuals to find their own methods of disposal. Composted wastes can be used again on parks, lawns, and gardens.

In addition, recycling reduces the amount of waste that is left to be incinerated or buried. We are running out of places to bury our garbage, with present landfills more and more difficult to come by. In the northeast and north central regions of the United States, landfills are said to have from five to ten years worth of space left. Even where there is space, nobody wants the garbage deposits next door. Incineration, which some claim to be safe, not only faces difficulty because of counterclaims about emissions but also because about 30 percent of the original waste is left as ash, with toxic possibilities.

The roughly 13 million tons of food disposed of in garbage would provide a substantial substitute for chemical fertilizers if some way could be found to separate it out. In some countries, this food waste is recovered, but no method has been devised to do this mechanically. The chief use of this type of waste has been in providing energy where nonrecyclables are incinerated.

Sewage wastes in some parts of the world are dumped into rivers, lakes, and oceans without treatment. Even in the United States, over 50 percent of the effluent (the water remaining after some treatment) contains nitrogen, phosphorous, and toxic metals and chemicals. Herbicides, insecticides, cadmium, and copper—all toxic—remain in the water, entering the food chain through fish and other marine life. Nitrogen and phosphorous help increase algae, which remove oxygen from water and thus prevent the growth of foods on which fish feed. In addition, there is the problem of disposing of the sludge that remains after treatment—about 30 percent of the original sewage volume.

Recently, according to an article in *Garbage,* several experiments in the natural or organic treatment of sewage have proven effective in producing purer effluent for less money (as compared to chemical treatment).[32] Essentially, the process uses plants and animals to remove the materials that have been added to water in the course of its use by humans and industries. Water hyacinths, cattails, calla lilies, algae, water iris, elephant ears, duckweed, snails, azalea, fern, bacteria, striped bass, and zooplankton are some of the life forms used in treatment. Chlorine is then used to kill the remaining danger, viruses. The result is water free of toxic substances—without any sludge. Thus far, only small communities, in which there is considerable space for the treatment plants, have tried this method. Such a plant consisting of 240 acres of ponds is located in Denham Springs, Louisiana, with the capacity to handle three million gallons of water serving twenty thousand persons.

Without question, natural methods are a big part of the future of sewage treatment. The results of releasing wastes only partially treated are seen in the two thousand square miles of dead water—without plant or animal life—at the mouth of the Mississippi. This suggests the need for what is called *tertiary* as well as *secondary* treatment, the former removing nitrogen, phosphorous, and toxic chemicals. The improved quality of the effluent, the reduction in costs, and the absence of residual sludge all argue for natural methods of treatment. How these methods can be made feasible for larger cities remains to be seen.

Economic Development in Developing Nations

Thus far we have looked at the ecological issues of global warming, ozone depletion, water conservation, and waste disposal. While none of these issues can be dealt with adequately without relating them to each other, we will continue to make more or less arbitrary distinctions. Such distinctions are more difficult to make in the case of Third World economic development. This issue involves poverty, land policies, income distribution patterns and political organizations in Third World nations, global warming, deforestation, land degradation and desertification, ozone depletion, international markets, population explosion, foreign aid policies, development philosophies, trade policies, agricultural policies, international financing institutions, debt relief, and the poisoning of exported food through the widespread use of pesticides.

The more I think about ecological issues, the more I see four basic problems: technologies that destroy natural and human processes and rhythms in the course of securing resources and producing products and by-products; economic systems that claim to be free from responsibility for the effects of their doctrines and practices; value systems that give priority to the products of these technologies; and political systems that in theory, or in practice, or both are unable to deal with the adverse consequences of the technologies and thus are in themselves destructive of the environment.

Many have suggested that developing nations cannot imitate the capitalist economic systems of the so-called developed nations without depleting essential resources and without causing such destruction to the natural world that human existence would be affected. Others claim that this system itself will solve most problems; for example, when resources begin to dwindle, prices will force a reconsideration of resource use such that those in short supply will be used less and thus will never be depleted. But with the lack of a market cost for the destruction of the natural world, I cannot see anything to stop us from sailing merrily along, waiting for the market to handle everything, until it is too late and we will be unable to develop technologies to reverse the destructive effects of ozone depletion or global warming. Two idols distort our vision: the idol of a market that automatically adjusts for the maximum benefit of all, and faith in our ability to respond to any problem created by humanity with a new technology.

In developed nations, destructive technologies are already in place and need to be changed or controlled either by political systems or by the votes of millions of consumers. Such change seems unlikely. There is little indication that the technologies of the developed world, in the hands of the world's corporate giants, will be thrown away for new technologies when the corporate giants extend their activities into developing nations. Nevertheless, it is in the long-term interests of both developing and developed nations to adopt new technologies in the developing nations, technologies with less damaging effects on the environment. Such technologies are available, but given market mechanisms and the mentalities of the chief players in the economic systems of all nations, it seems unlikely that the incentives for using them will function in the market system. At present, developing nations interpret the advocacy of more friendly technologies as the haves telling the have-nots to use less competitive, less productive technologies while they, the developed nations, continue to indulge in destructive technologies. There is no easy way to deal with this issue. In spite of growing awareness, it is almost inconceivable that the developed nations will reduce their carbon emissions by even half of the 80 percent that some feel is necessary. How, then, can we suggest that developing nations establish policies that do not increase their emissions, emissions that represent a much less developed industrial base? In 1988, North American carbon emissions were at the rate of 5.07 tons per person, compared to 2.09 tons per person in Latin America, .86 tons per person in Africa, .55 tons per person in the Far East, and .66 tons per person in Asia. These developing areas will likely be the places in which 95 percent of the expected population increase of 3.5 billion persons is expected by 2040.[33]

If the use of fossil fuels, the basis of the economic expansion of the industrial societies, were to continue at the present rate of increase of 3 percent per year, the carbon emissions from the use of fossil fuels in the world would be more that 25 billion tons by 2040—about five times the present rate. Or, if we use the predicted population by 2040 of 9 billion people and assume the average emission rate will be just twice the present rate of 1.42 tons per person (including deforestation and fossil fuel use), emissions will still be more than 25 billion tons annually. At the North American 1990 rate of 5.07 tons per person, emissions in 2040 would be 45 billion tons, or nine times the present rate. Even if we assume that these emissions will have a modest effect on global warming, such a situation is unacceptable to anyone who cares about the future. A program of economic development in the developing nations that uses the current technology of the developed nations is suicidal. Third World patterns of economic development must become one of the absolutely essential concerns of every person in the world.[34]

The current reduction in the size of forests in developing nations is a crucial aspect of Third World economic development. To reduce the forests is to reduce the number of trees that absorb carbon dioxide in their growth and thus to increase the amount of carbon dioxide available to cause the greenhouse effect. Fast-growing hardwoods absorb about 6 tons of carbon per hectare and are responsible for about .5 tons more retained in the soil. In 1980, carbon emissions from deforestation were estimated to be 1.7 billion tons. This includes both the carbon dioxide given off in the burning of forests as well as the amount not absorbed by growing trees and the soil protected by the trees. This probably means that a substantial amount of the total estimated 1988 carbon emissions of 7.3 trillion tons came from forest reduction. In 1980, at least two-thirds of the emissions from forest degradation came from developing nations.[35] Thus any program designed to reduce the threat of global warming from carbon emissions involves the policies of developing nations regarding forest destruction, economic policies that lead poor citizens to slash and burn forests to get access to land for the sake of subsistence crops or that encourage large-scale enterprises to develop exportable crops or other products produced on deforested land. Costa Rica, for example, has only 17 percent of its forests left. In many developing nations, huge cattle ranches have been developed to provide cheap beef for U.S. fast-food chains. One study claims that forty-five square feet of forest are destroyed and desertified for every hamburger produced.[36]

In addition, wood also plays a major role in providing the persons of developing nations with energy. According to Worldwatch, wood's share of the total energy use in six African nations runs between 71 and 98 percent; in India, 33 percent; in Indonesia, 50 percent; in Nepal, 94 percent; in Brazil, 20 percent; in Costa Rica, 33 percent; in Nicaragua, 50 percent; and in Paraguay, 64 percent. In 1980, there was an acute shortage of wood for 49 million persons in tropical Africa, 29 million persons in tropical Asia, and 18 million persons in tropical America. The minimum fuel needs were met by overcutting and depleting wood resources for 200 million persons in tropical Africa, 710 million persons in tropical Asia, and 143 million persons in tropical America. Predictions for the year 2000 estimate acute scarcity or deficits for 622 million persons in tropical Africa, 434 million persons in tropical Asia, and 342 million persons in tropical America.[37]

The pressures leading to deforestation and thus to the threat of global warming and a lack of fuel come from the population explosion, from concentrated land ownership patterns, from internal economic organization, from transnational corporations that foster land use for export crops, from economic policies and practices that lead to huge external debt and high interest payments, and from economic policies that depress the price of the developing nations' products on the world market.

The world's population increased by 88 million in 1989 and is predicted to rise by 96 million per year in the nineties. This means that by the year 2000 the population will be 6.3 billion—an increase of 959 million in the nineties. If we then project to the year 2040 at the rate of 100 million per year, the population will be 10.3 billion, or roughly twice what it is today. This presumes that there is no increase in the rate of population growth (most of this growth is expected in the developing nations). With increasing attention to the population issue, growth rates might be expected to decline, but experience in countries with very aggressive programs, such as China, indicate that while the rate of growth may be slowed, the population will continue to increase.

With the growth in population, the pressure on all natural resources will increase dramatically. Some contend that raising the levels of women's education, economic opportunities, and status, in addition to easy access to birth control resources, lowers birth rates. Studies also indicate that many women in developing countries do not want large families. But without dramatic changes in the economic conditions of developing nations, changes in women's status are unlikely. Today we have 1.2 billion persons living in absolute poverty (the absence of minimal food, clothing, and housing resources), so there is little that suggests a leveling off of the population—except death from hunger and related diseases.

Land ownership patterns in many developing nations, where agriculture is so central to earning a living, work against a rational program for land use. Most of the land, and practically all of the good land, is in the hands of a few wealthy elites. Peasants are forced to exploit poorer and poorer land or forests, without regard to the consequences. For example, in the Dominican Republic, 48 percent of the population are nearly land less, and 44 percent are landless; in Guatemala, 47 percent are nearly landless, and 38 percent are landless; in Ecuador, 52 percent are nearly landless, and 23 percent are landless; in Peru, 46 percent are nearly land less, and 29 percent are landless; in Brazil, 10 percent are nearly landless, and 60 percent are landless; in the Philippines, 34 percent are nearly land less, and 35 percent are landless; in Colombia, 24 percent are nearly land less, and 42 percent are landless; in El Salvador, 65 percent are landless; in Honduras, 46 percent are nearly landless, and 18 percent are landless.[38] In Venezuela, 1 percent of the landholders own 67 percent of the land; in Colombia, 1 percent own 48 percent of the land; in Brazil, fifteen families own 45 percent of the land; in Honduras, 1 percent own 48 percent of the land; in Mexico, 2 percent own 47 percent of the land.[39]

Typically, the average poor person in a developing nation is not a subsistence farmer but a dispossessed laborer. The degradation of the land has resulted in the displacement of laborers; the mechanization of agriculture has resulted in the displacement of millions more. Developing nations caught with rising populations, land degradation, and large-scale unemployment have borrowed huge sums from developed nations—$1.3 trillion by 1989—and thus face pressures to increase their production of export crops and to build the infrastructures that support economic development: roads, schools, health facilities, and high-technology equipment. Dependent as they are on the price of their exportable products in the world markets, they are at the mercy of developed nations, which can subsidize the income of their farmers while they dump surpluses on the world markets, thus depressing prices. For example, between 1980 and 1987, the prices of the products on which most developing nations are dependent for foreign exchange, such as copper, iron ore, timber, sugar, coffee, and cotton, fell 40 percent on the average. During 1986 and 1987, the United States dumped a surplus of rice on the world market, driving down the price from eight dollars per hundred pounds to four dollars per hundred pounds. While the U.S. government made up the difference to its 19,000 rice farmers, 4 million Thai farmers absorbed the loss in income. Critics state that the farm subsidy program of the United States undermines the economic development of Third World nations. Subsidizing our agriculture increases production to the extent that it depresses prices on the world markets, thus decreasing incentives and incomes for farmers in developing nations. Price supports thus allow our farmers to compete unfairly in world markets.

Worldwatch Institute argues that the net result of poverty in the developing nations will be increased deaths due to starvation and disease, increased destruction of food-producing resources due to overuse, increased defaults on interest and loan payments due to the use of exportable food resources to counter starvation, and increased pressure on developed nations to help their financial institutions refinance and forgive loans.

Thus there can be no questions that Third World economic development, with its implications for global warming, ozone depletion, mass starvation, and political stability, is of major significance for all nations. Such development is tied to sustainable world economic development. The scope of the challenge is suggested by estimates on the money required to address Third World economic problems during the 1990s: for protecting topsoil on cropland, $114 billion; for reforestation, $32 billion; for slowing the rate of population growth, $159 billion; for raising energy efficiency, $180 billion; for developing renewable energy, $94 billion; for retiring the debt of developing countries, $150 billion. These sums, totaling some $834 billion, do not seem large in the face of the roughly $1 trillion a year that has been spent worldwide for military affairs recently.[40]

Population Explosion

The growth of the population, predicted to be as much as 100 million persons per year in the 1990s, will result in millions of deaths from hunger and related diseases (more than the 60 million persons per year die of such causes at present). The radical reallocation of the resources of the world, especially of the developed world, is essential if we are not to make a mockery of religious traditions, which claim that we are responsible for taking care of brothers and sisters, and if we do not want to become so insensitive to death that life everywhere becomes cheap. Spending $1 trillion a year worldwide on military development and using 80 percent of the U.S. corn crop and 95 percent of the U.S. oats crop by cycling grain through livestock (thus wasting 90 percent of the protein and 99 percent of the fiber of these grains) are impossible to justify.

All the ecological problems that we have considered thus far are compounded by the population explosion. The population explosion leads to great stresses on the food, fuel, water, mineral, and housing supply; air quality; forest degradation; health, education, and waste disposal facilities; transportation; political stability; and racial and religious tensions.

In 1960, planet earth had 3 billion persons; in 1990, 5.292 billion. The population is doubling every 38 years. By 2025, we can expect 8.456 billion persons in the world, roughly 1.6 billion in the developed nations and 6.84 billion in the developing nations, unless some unexpected biological or social tragedy wipes out huge segments. AIDS may develop by epidemic proportions; a nuclear war could drastically if not permanently interrupt the population explosion. The population of the United States is predicted to rise from 249.2 million persons in 1990 to 300.8 million persons in 2025; Mexico, from 88.6 million in 1990 to 150.1 million in 2025. Imagine for a moment what the Rio Grande River border will be like in 2025 unless drastic changes occur in the economic and social life of Mexico.

By 2025, the population in El Salvador will increase from 5.3 million persons in 1990 to 11.3 million; in Guatemala, from 9.2 to 21.7 million; in Nicaragua, from 3.9 to 9.2 million; in Panama, from 2.4 to 3.9 million. If development in Central America has been an issue in the past, it will be even more an issue in the future.

By 2025, the population in Nigeria will increase from 113 to 301.3 million persons; in Ethiopia, from 46.7 to 112.3 million; in Egypt, from 54.1 to 94 million; in South Africa, from 35.2 to 63.2 million; in Kenya, from 25.1 to 77.6 million; in Zaire, from 36.0 to 99.5 million; in Tanzania, from 27.3 to 84.8 million; in Brazil, from 150.4 to 345.8 million; in Colombia, from 31.8 to 51.7 million; in Bangladesh, from 115.6 to 235.0 million; in China, from 1.1 to 1.5 billion; in India, from 853.4 million to 1.4 billion; in Iran, from 56.6 to 122.2 million; in Iraq, from 18.9 to 50.0 million; in Kuwait, from 300,000 to 2.1 million; in Israel, from 4.6 to 6.9 million; in Jordan, from 4.3 to 13.1 million; in Pakistan, from 122.7 to 267.1 million; in Vietnam, from 67.2 to 118.0 million; in the Philippines, from 62.4 to 111.4 million. European countries generally will lose population or gain very little during the next thirty-five years.[41]

The implications of the population rise in these particular countries reinforce the devastating conviction that the developing world is in for trouble. More than 95 percent of the roughly 3.2-billion-person increase in population will be in the developing nations, where resources for caring for present populations are already strained and where millions of persons are dying of starvation and hunger-related diseases each year. It is estimated that 40,000 children under the age of five die of hunger and hunger-related diseases every day; 60 million persons of all ages die of hunger and hunger-related diseases every year.

Resources in developing countries are already in short supply. Some predict that the hectares of land per person in food production in Third World countries will decrease from .45 in 1950 to .23 in 2000, while for the developed nations the decrease will be from .60 to .48. Total grain production will decrease from .23 hectares per person in 1950 to .12 in 2000. Per capita world grain production will decline in the 1990s by 16 percent.[42] Persons deficient in fuel wood will probably increase from 249 million to 622 million by 2000 in tropical Africa, from 739 million in 1.4 billion in tropical Asia, and from 161 million to 342 million in tropical America.[43] Twenty-three percent of the persons in the world live in absolute poverty, that is, without minimal food, clothing, and housing: 675 million persons in Asia (25 percent of the population); 325 million in sub-Saharan Africa (62 percent of the population); 150 million in Latin America (35 percent of the population); and 75 million in northern Africa and the Middle East (28 percent of the population).[44] This is before the population explosion of the next thirty-five years, with the expected increase of 3.3 billion persons in these areas.[45]

This population increase is a threat to the integrity of Christian spirituality and of any spirituality that affirms that humankind is in some sense a whole, a community, a related reality. It undermines the notion that there is any mutuality involved in being human. It makes a mockery of any belief that we are each other's keeper. It threatens to make human life so cheap that all life will lose any sense of sacredness—if this has not already happened with the manufacture of weapons that can wipe out millions of persons indiscriminately.

The population explosion threatens to deplete what limited resources many Third World countries already possess. The estimated losses of forest lands in nine countries due to farming or grazing, huge ranches for livestock, lumbering, and roads and industrial development are as follows: Vietnam, 427,000 acres per year; Thailand, 981,000 acres; the Philippines, 853,000 acres; Myanamar, 1.9 million acres; Indonesia, 2.2 million acres; India, 3.7 million acres; Costa Rica, 306,000 acres; Cameroon, 247,000 acres; Brazil, 19.8 million acres. The meaning of this forest destruction for species extinction; for removing trees that use carbon dioxide and thus reduce the global warming threat; for preventing soil erosion, flooding, and the loss of life; for providing fuel and economic income on a sustained basis (rubber tapping in Brazil or tourism in Kenya, for example); and for recreation staggers the imagination.

The population explosion puts a strain on the political stability of many Third World countries, some of which are already in the midst of struggles between the haves and the have-nots. This can only be exacerbated. Political explosions will increase and will have reverberations throughout the world as developed nations seek to defend their interests— both economic and ideological. We can expect more interventions and larger budgets in developed nations for international aid, both military and economic. I have already alluded to the problem the United States will face on its southern border as the populations of Central and South American countries increase by at least 80 percent by 2025. The end of the cold war will make future U.S. interventions to protect naked economic interests more divisive at home and abroad. The inability of Third World social systems to provide for their added population will increase the intensity of the ideological struggle between the dominant economic and political institutions and some new approach to meeting the needs of millions of starving persons.

The population explosion in the United States, while limited to 20 percent (a rise from 249 million persons to 300 million), will accentuate our disproportionate use of natural resources. With only 4.7 percent of the world's population, the United States emits at least 20 percent of the global warming gases and uses about 25 percent of the world's resources; for example, we use over 6 billion barrels of oil out of the 24 billion barrels used worldwide each year. The pressure of the environmental movement will be on us, pointing to the irresponsibility in our policies regarding population growth in light of the disproportionate amount of damage done to the environment by each citizen of the United States.

The population explosion will make unmistakably clear that the style of life to which the developed nations have become accustomed will no longer be possible without a new approach to world relations. The lifestyle of the developed countries cannot be universalized; that is, it cannot work in a world of ten or fifteen billion persons. The only way for developed nations to preserve their present lifestyle will be to form fortified castles of their nations—largely self-sufficient economies not threatened either by the superior technologies or the low wages of other countries. This isolationism, of course, is exactly opposite to what is advocated by our elite economists, corporate leaders, and policymakers in Washington. Even this "world economy" may be impossible when one examines the essential resource requirements of the developed economies. Just how important certain minerals are for the developed countries' style of life is not clear. A chart showing the import dependencies of the European Economic Community, Japan, and United States indicates that all of these entities are heavily dependent on imports for most of the thirty-seven important non-fuel minerals. The United States is independent in twenty-three cases for 40 percent or more of its supply. The European Community is dependent for more than 40 percent in twenty-five cases. Japan is dependent in twenty-nine cases for 66 percent or more.[46] Just how Third World countries can use their resources to bargain with the developed nations is somewhat evident in the case of OPEC. What it might cost us to prevent being cut off from essential resources is not clear. It is clear that the future world is going to be quite different from the old "new world." The stakes are different. Everyone is hurt by the population explosion.

So what is to be done? Most studies indicate that if women are given a chance to get an education, participate in a stable economic system, achieve higher status, and gain access to and education about birth control methods, the birthrate will go down. If we look at Third World countries in which significant reductions in the average annual increase in population have been achieved, we find that the annual rate of increase has gone down in Thailand from 2.44 percent in the period 1975–80 to 1.53 percent in 1985–90; in Guinea-Bissau, from 5.04 percent to 2.08 percent during the same periods; in Sri-Lanka, from 1.71 percent to 1.32 percent. On the average, African countries have gone from 2.63 percent in the period from 1965–70 to 2.95 percent in 1975–80 to 3.00 percent in 1985–90; Asian countries, from 2.44 percent to 1.86 percent to 1.85 percent. This, of course, includes China, which went from 2.61 percent to 1.43 percent to 1.39 percent; India, which went from 2.28 percent to 2.08 percent to 2.08 percent; Japan, which went from 1.07 percent to .93 percent to .44 percent; and Indonesia, which went from 2.33 percent to 2.14 percent to 1.62 percent. In the meantime, the United States went from 1.08 percent to 1.06 percent to .82 percent. Even in the case of Thailand, which is held up as a model in the "Race to Save the Planet" video,[47] the population is predicted to rise from 55.7 million persons in 1990 to 80.9 million in 2025. The government of Thailand, like the government of China, has taken a very active and dramatic lead in working for lower birth rates. In the case of China, the radical steps taken during their period of rigid centralization of authority resulted in a reduction of the average annual population change from 2.61 percent in 1965–70 to 1.43

percent in 1975–80 to 1.39 percent in 1985–90. Still, the increase in population is predicted to be from 1.1 billion in 1990 to 1.5 billion in 2025. I cannot imagine any more drastic measures for population control than were taken in China. Clearly, the world—and I mean all persons and their governments everywhere—has a great stake in what is happening in countries where populations are increasing at a rate of more than .25 percent a year—which includes all countries except those in Europe. The average growth rate in Europe in 1985–90 was .23 percent per year, with population growth projections from 497.7 million persons in 1990 to 512.3 million in 2025. The average growth rate in the world in 1985–90 was 1.73 percent. The average in Africa was 3.00 percent, from 647.5 million persons in 1990 to 1.6 billion in 2025; in North and Central America, the average was 1.28 percent, from 427.2 million persons in 1990 to 594.9 million in 2020; in Asia, the average growth rate was 1.85 percent, from 3.1 billion persons in 1990 to 4.9 billion in 2025. The growth rate in Oceania was 1.44 percent, with population growth from 26.5 million persons in 1990 to 39 million in 2025.[48]

Paul and Anne Ehrlich, in the Winter 1990 edition of *Amicus,* assert that if persons everywhere today ate as Americans do, there would only be enough in the record harvests of 1985 and 1986 to feed half of the present world population. What if the one-third of the grain harvest of the United States now fed to animals were available for direct human consumption? Then, perhaps a billion more people could be fed by the 1986 harvest. While the maldistribution of food today is a real issue, food distribution tomorrow will be an even bigger problem given current rates of population growth.

The population explosion—along with its implications for starvation and for political and economic theory and practice—and the threat of global warming are clearly the two most important issues facing the world today.

Loss of Soil, Cropland, Crops, Forests, Species, Clean Air, and Minerals

Clearly, we are losing resources that we have been given, that are not easily replaceable, and that, in some cases, are irreplaceable. We are using up humankind's inheritance. Future generations will not be given the resources that our generation has had. The overall impression one gets from this state of loss is that the present generation is irresponsible. We will either become responsible for and to the future, or we will deny ourselves a future—and thus deny our connection to each other and to a God who embraces and cares for the future as well as the present.

Loss of Soil, Cropland, and Crops

One-third of the world's cropland is being degraded by the loss of twenty-four billion tons of topsoil every year. The erosion is the result of the destruction of forests and the resulting rapid runoff of rainwater; the overgrazing of fields; the increased planting of fields to meet the needs of exploding populations; planting without regard for the techniques that provide for the growth of topsoil; and changing climate patterns that result in droughts in some areas and heavy rains in others.

The degradation of land in the late seventies was estimated to be severe (more than 50 percent degraded) in 17 percent of African cropland, 16 percent of Asian, 7 percent of Australian, 6 percent of European, 7 percent of North American, and 10 percent of South American cropland. Moderate degradation of 10 to 50 percent affected about 23 percent of cropland in Africa, 28 percent in Asia, 55 percent in Australia, 25 percent in Europe, 23 percent in North America, and 17 percent in South America.[49]

A U.S. study estimates that the loss of crops due to soil erosion is 6 percent for every inch of topsoil lost. Worldwide, this erosion results in the loss of 9 million tons of grain and 24 billion tons of topsoil each year.[50]

Otherwise usable soil is degraded by waterlogging and by salt residues that remain when irrigated land is not drained properly. Some estimate that this degradation affects 24 percent of the world's 180 million acres of grain cropland and results in the loss of 1.1 million tons of grain.[51]

Grain crop yields are reduced by another 2 million tons by the loss of fertilizer when cow dung is burned for fuel because of increasing deforestation; by the shortening of cultivation cycles because of the pressures of increasing populations; and by the compaction of the soil due to the use of heavy equipment.[52]

In addition, losses in crops occur because of air pollution from sulfur dioxide, nitrous oxide, and especially ozone (at low levels). This accounts for another 1 million tons of grain lost. Flooding, acid rain, and increased ultraviolet radiation are said to result in the loss of another 1 million tons of grain.

Thus, in total there is a loss of about 14 million tons of grain, which, when subtracted from the increase in production of about 29 million tons a year, leaves us with 15 million tons of additional grain to meet the estimated 28-million-ton increase required yearly to meet the needs of the increasing population.[53]

This, of course, assumes that growing conditions remain relatively constant—a large assumption in light of the fact that in 1988, grain production was off from 1987 levels in the United States by 74 million tons, in the Soviet Union by 16 million tons, and in China by 7 million tons. If the predicted climate shifts associated with global warming do materialize, one cannot be optimistic about the capacity of the existing soils to produce enough food to feed the people of the world.[54]

Projections of world grain production are 1.7 billion tons for 1990 and 1.8 billion tons for 2000, with changes in the decades being + 34 percent in the 1960s, + 30 percent in the 1970s, + 31 percent in the 1980s, + 17 percent in the 1990s, and + 9 percent in the 2000s. The world population will probably increase by 18 percent during that decade, but the grain per capita available will decrease by 7 percent, from 316 kilograms per capita to 295 kilograms per capita. At a time when world population is predicted to rise dramatically, the increase in productivity due to the heavy use of fertilizers and new strains of grain crops during the last decades is predicted to end, with only modest gains in productivity. This means only one thing: increases in food shortages and starvation. If 60 million people died in 1990 (as estimated) due to hunger and hunger-related diseases, we can expect that figure to increase dramatically during the rest of the decade and beyond. The total cropland under cultivation began to fall from 724 million hectares in 1980 to 720 million hectares in 1990. The amount of irrigated land continues to increase, from 188 million hectares in 1970, 236 million hectares in 1980, 259 million hectares in 1990, and a projected 279 million hectares in 2000.[55] The threats that this irrigation poses to the water supply in the form of the waterlogging and the increased salinity of soils and lakes have already been discussed.

One prediction of the future situation shows the total arable land available for production dropping while the land needed at present productive levels increases with the increase in population; the curves cross about the year 2000, which suggests a dramatic increase in hunger-related problems. If the level of productivity per hectare were doubled, the curves would cross about 2020, and if the level of productivity were quadrupled, the curves would cross about 2050.[56]

Loss of Forests

The world's forests provide vast quantities of marketable timber, pulp, and fuel wood. Hundreds of millions of people depend on wood for cooking and heating. In addition, the forests play a role in preventing soil erosion, in affecting climate, in taking carbon dioxide out of the atmosphere, in preventing flooding, and in providing homes and marketable crops (nuts, rubber, fruits) for forest people.

Originally covering about 6.2 billion hectares (1 hectare is 2.47 acres), the clearing of forests for crop production, for raising cattle, and for commercial uses has reduced the world's forested area by about one-third. Estimates vary, but tropical forests are said to represent about 25 percent of the total loss, somewhere around 1.6 billion hectares originally, now down to between 800 to 900 million hectares. Some estimate that tropical forests are losing about 10 million hectares each year, the difference between the loss of 11 million and the planting of 1 million hectares. The ratio in Africa is 29 hectares cleared for every 1 hectare planted; in Asia, 5 hectares are cleared for every 1 planted.[57]

Industrial pollution resulting in acid rain has led to extensive forest damage, especially in the developed nations. In Europe's forests, about 50 million hectares out of about 140 million—about 35 percent—have been damaged.[58]

We are losing our forests, and while, here and there, heroic steps have been made to prevent further losses, the world is yet to awake to the consequences of the failure to deal with these losses.

In the Third World, about two-thirds of the persons are dependent on fuel wood for their cooking and heating.[59] About 70 percent of the total energy used comes from wood. Researchers predict acute shortages or the use of fuel wood in such a way as to deplete the resources for the future for about 2.4 billion persons by the year 2000, 622 million persons in tropical Africa, 1.4 billion persons in tropical Asia, and 342 million persons in Latin America. Some estimate that developing nations, not including China, will have to plant 55 million hectares of trees between 1980 and 2000 to prevent serious consequences for fuel wood supplies alone.[60]

Industrial wood is in better supply, especially since it is provided in large part by the developed nations.[61] However, increasing needs for logs, pulp, and other raw materials for wood products threaten to create such a demand that Third World tropical forests will be pillaged for wood without the benefit of managed policies of logging and replanting. Already, Nigerian exports of hardwood have declined from 773,000 cubic meters in 1964 to 60,000 cubic meters from 1976–85 due to exploitation. Nigeria exported $6 million and imported $160 million of forest products in 1985. One potential problem involves the developed nations raising the tariffs on imported processed wood when and if developing nations attempt to reap the benefits from processing their own wood. Some Third World countries (Brazil, Nigeria, Indonesia, Chile, Zimbabwe, and Zambia) have thus instituted industrial forest plantation projects.[62] But of the about 92 million hectares of industrial forest plantations in 1985, about 74.5 million hectares were in the former USSR (21.9 million), China (17.5 million), the United States (12.1 million), Japan (9.6 million), and Western Europe (13 million).[63]

The loss of forests affects soil and water resources, causing fast run-offs, flooding, and the uneven availability of water for crops and hydroelectric power plants where storage reservoirs are not available. It also increases the filling of rivers and reservoirs with silt, thus further affecting the hydroelectric power generated. Wind erosion also leads to silt buildup in bodies of water. Sedimentation rates in two reservoirs in the Philippines increased 105 and 121 percent from 1967 to 1980, for example.[64]

The loss of forests is also a factor in the rate of global warming. The burning of forests contributes billions of tons of carbon dioxide to the atmosphere. For example, researchers estimate that the burning of tropical forests in 1980 in Brazil alone contributed 336 million tons of carbon. In 1980, the world emissions of carbon from tropical deforestation were 1.7 billion tons.[65]

Some predict that the increase in carbon dioxide in the atmosphere and the resulting increase in global temperatures will increase the rate of respiration in all plants, thus increasing the amount of carbon dioxide even more. This could cause plants and trees to engage in less photosynthesis than respiration, the imbalance leading to deterioration. Others predict that warmer climates mean more decomposition of organic matter, more food for plants and trees, and more use of carbon dioxide, thus offsetting the effects of the carbon dioxide produced by fossil fuel use and by the burning of forests.

Whatever the ultimate effect, it is certain that the reduction in the number of trees results in a reduction in the amount of carbon dioxide used in their photosynthesis, thus contributing to global-warming trends. Somewhere between 2 and 6.5 tons of carbon dioxide are absorbed by the average tree. Trees in the tropics grow about twice as fast as those in the temperate climates, and different varieties grow at different rates and absorb different amounts. To remove the trees is to remove this capacity to absorb carbon dioxide; to plant trees is to provide this absorbing capacity. Thus, programs that lead to millions of hectares of trees in the tropics make sense. In the mid-1980s, some experts pushed for the planting of about 20 billion trees annually to reach a goal of some 125 million hectares of new plantings by 2000.

One estimate found Europe and possibly Japan and South Korea as the only regions in which the total plant life took in more carbon dioxide than was given off in respiration and deforestation.[66] Europe's forests, as we have discussed, are threatened with air pollution and acid rain.

All kinds of programs are underway at all levels to meet the crisis of our forests. What is possible depends on the resources available, the leadership of national governments and international agencies, the state of local and world economies, the pressures from the population explosion, the ingenuity of local leaders, and the communication of successful programs to million of persons.

Loss of Species

Connected with the loss of forests is the loss of thousands of species whose habitat is the forest. We are also losing species in other habitats, such as in lakes and oceans that have become inhospitable to life.

The loss of about 45 percent of our tropical forests means the loss of a certain percentage of the species located there, estimated to be about half of the species for each ten-fold decrease in area.[67] Estimates of the number of species extant worldwide run from 10 to 30 million, with 1.4 million having been given biological names. A good portion of the extant species are in the tropical forests. So, if we have lost 45 percent of the tropical forests, which may contain 80 percent of the 10 to 30 million total species worldwide, we have lost a good number of species. One estimate puts the present rate of loss of tropical forests at 1 percent per year and the loss of species at from .2 to .3 percent per year. Deforestation is responsible for the loss of from 4,000 to 6,000 species a year, by some estimates. This loss is said to be as much as ten thousand times greater than normal expectations from nonhuman causes.

One of the real resources of the planet earth is its biological diversity, created over millions of years. Students of these matters note that over the last 600 million years there have been several periods in which mass extinctions have occurred. Some 52 percent of extant species were lost about 240 million years ago, for example. Increasingly, we have discovered that a variety of species can provide new foods, new medicines (such as rosy periwinkle, used to treat Hodgkin's disease and acute lymphocyte leukemia), new fibers and petroleum substitutes, and oil for cooking and many, many more discoveries to come.

The general conclusion of biologists is that we are squandering a gene pool with resources so vast and complicated that we have not yet begun to understand its value.

Loss of Clean Air

We have always assumed that air was available for the breathing and the using and that it was so limitless that we could fill it with all kinds of things without affecting its usefulness, except in the case of a few obvious poisons. Now we are learning that there are all kinds of consequences for what we put into the air.

We have already seen the results of filling the air with all kinds of gases: carbon dioxide, chlorofluorocarbons, methane, nitrous oxide—all of which we now know are causing the average global temperature to increase, with potentially disastrous consequences. We have also learned how chlorofluorocarbons, methyl chloroform, carbon tetrachloride, and halons are responsible for the reduction of ozone in the stratosphere and thus for the increase of ultraviolet rays reaching the earth, with predicted negative effects on the health of humans, plants, and animals.

In this section we will look at the way in which sulfur oxides, nitrogen oxides, hydrocarbons, carbon monoxide, particulates, and lead are responsible for increasing the risk of certain health hazards—cancer, genetic defects, and respiratory diseases—and for exacerbating heart and lung diseases. The chief culprits are electric generating plants, industrial plants generally, and motor vehicles.

Broadly speaking, there are two approaches to rectifying this situation and reducing the related threats. On the one hand, we can remove the offending gases and particles from the processes that produce them. On the other hand, we can make drastic changes in our current energy, transportation, and industrial systems.

From the beginning, we need to recognize that the air is sending us a message about the way we fail to focus on the consequences of human activities. We need some Band-Aids, but they will not do the entire job. We seem to be having a difficult time getting our leaders to accept the fact that there is a problem. But persons living or working in downtown Los Angeles, Mexico City, or any one of a number of cities—New Delhi, Xi'an, Beijing, Shenyang, Tehran, São Paulo, Ankara, Melbourne—know what it means to live with unhealthy air. Los Angeles has considered banning cars from the downtown area altogether. We simply use too much gasoline and too much energy, and we permit industry to spew forth too much toxic waste into the air. In the summer of 1988, 150 million people in the United States were exposed for at least 1 day to levels of ozone that exceed acceptable federal standards; persons in Los Angeles were exposed for 178 days. In Mexico City, seven out of ten babies had lead levels above the

World Health Organization's acceptable levels when they were born. In one area in West Virginia—an area with thirteen major chemical plants—respiratory cancer was 21 percent above the national average. These isolated situations illustrate only a fraction of the problems caused by the loss of clean air.

The same industrial processes and transportation policies that produce the pollutants affecting human health also produce the pollutants that affect the natural environment. These pollutants are causing the deterioration of buildings and monuments to the tune of billions of dollars. Sulfur and nitrogen oxides from fossil fuel (oil, gasoline, natural gas) combustion damage lungs and the respiratory tract; make streams, lakes, and soils acidic and thus inhospitable to life; eat away at buildings and materials; and, along with ozone, kill millions of acres of trees. Carbon monoxide, chiefly from motor vehicles, affects the ability of the blood to carry oxygen to the pulmonary, nervous, and respiratory systems. It helps also in ozone formation. Volatile organic compounds from vehicles and industry sometimes cause cancer or mutations and contribute to ozone formation. Ozone itself, formed from the interactions of nitrogen oxides and organic compounds in the atmosphere, causes eye irritation, nasal congestion, and asthma as well as affecting other aspects of the respiratory system; it also makes infections more likely.

These emissions also harm trees and plants. Air pollution has affected 35 percent of the trees in Europe. Crop losses due to ozone are also reported: 1 percent or less for sorghum and corn, 7 percent for cotton and soybeans, and more than 30 percent for alfalfa. Who is responsible for the estimated five or six billion dollar crop loss?[68]

What can be done? Generally speaking, we have two broad alternatives, pollution control or pollution prevention.

In the first case, national and international programs are pushing for the use of scrubbers and filters to reduce the amount of sulfur oxides emitted by power plants. As of 1987, 20 percent of U.S. coal-fired power plants had scrubbers, and there were plans for 30 percent by 2000. By way of contrast, in 1987, 30 percent of what were then West German power plants had scrubbers, with plans for 85 percent by 2000; Sweden had 50 percent of its plants equipped with scrubbers; Austria had 60 percent; Japan 85 percent. Italy's goal was 70 percent; the Netherlands's goal was 100 percent.

Nitrogen oxides can be reduced by improved combustion processes (30 to 50 percent effective) or by catalytic devices, with 80 to 90 percent effectiveness. Japan had about 54 percent of its coal-burning facilities equipped with these devices at the end of 1986. The United States has invested in the first approach. New plants are generally controlled in the developed countries, but retrofitting has been pursued significantly only by Denmark, the Netherlands, Germany, Sweden, and the United Kingdom.[69]

It is striking that the United States seems to be dragging its feet in recognizing that there are very serious problems with air pollution. For example, recently an intergovernmental panel conducting Climate Change, a gigantic cooperative study by hundreds of scientists and policymakers, released the reports of three of its working groups. According to the Fall/Winter 1990 newsletter of the Rocky Mountain Institute, "The first, chaired by Britain, confirmed that global warming is a real threat. Another, chaired by the Soviet Union, showed that global warming would be very harmful. And a third, chaired by the United States, claimed that little can or should be done to prevent it." Since then, our leaders have believed that there is little that can or should be done, and there has been little movement among our policymakers to address the scope of the issues. It is obvious that with the Clinton-Gore administration we have a fundamental shift both in awareness of the seriousness of environmental issues and in the willingness of the government to intervene in and set conditions for the market.

On the other hand, private groups—such as a new Energy Foundation sponsored by the Rockefeller Foundation, the John D. and Catherine T. MacArthur Foundation, and the Pew Charitable Trust of Philadelphia —have united on projects to help us save between 30 and 50 percent of the energy we consume annually. Likewise, the class of 1955 at Princeton has adopted as a long-term class project the task of persuading U.S. citizens and leaders that energy efficiency is a sure winner for everybody. Had these moves taken place after the OPEC crisis in the seventies, we would have little need for any imported oil today.

Of course, Amory and Hunter Lovins, with their Rocky Mountain Institute, have been leading the world in this direction ever since Amory published his "The Soft Energy Path."[70]

Lessening air pollution involves improving energy efficiency, taxing the use of fossil fuels to reduce their use, recycling, changing our transportation systems, and above all, limiting the disposal of polluting substances into land, air, and water. But air pollution is an issue involving something more than new technology reluctantly forced on an unwilling, resisting America. As I have argued elsewhere, it is a matter of both doing things as efficiently as we are capable of doing them and living our lives, both collectively and individually, in ways that do not require the excessive use of resources without regard to the cost.

Loss of Minerals—Fuels

The amount of known oil reserves as of 1989, according to the British Petroleum Statistical Review, was 1 trillion barrels.[71] The worldwide annual use of oil as of the first two months of 1990 was reported at about 22.4 billion barrels.[72] We thus have roughly forty-five years of oil at the present rate of production and use. Even if we double the estimated amount of reserves, we will have only ninety years of oil at recent rates of use. There are very few who predict that use will decline. According to some 1989 estimates, Middle Eastern countries are sitting on top of 660 billion barrels, or roughly 65 percent of the known reserves.[73] One frequently sees 70 percent as the figure given for the Arab share of reserves. U.S. reserves are estimated at 27 billion barrels according to the *United States of America National Report,* prepared for the United Nations Conference on Environment and Development. U.S. consumption of oil is about 6 billion barrels per year, with the percentage of imported oil rising recently to about 7.1 million barrels per day, or about 2.6 billion barrels per year.[74] Most likely, we will produce less and less oil domestically and become more and more dependent on imports.

It is in light of this situation, of course, that energy-efficiency advocates make their case of greatly increased mileage standards for cars—63 percent of our oil is used for transportation. With about 250 million people, the United States uses about 6 billion barrels of oil each year, or about 24 barrels per person. If the world's more than 5 billion people used oil at the same rate, we would use 120 billion barrels per year. At that rate, we would have less than ten years of oil left.

More importantly, not only do we not have enough oil to continue its use at anywhere near the present levels, but the use of the oil results in the production of carbon dioxide, which one *must* assume is a risk that cannot be tolerated. The more I read about global warming, the more I am convinced that we ignore this problem at our peril.

It is important to recognize the extent to which the countries of the world depend on imports of energy.[75] Japan, for example, depends on oil for 58 percent of its energy and imports all of it, amounting in 1989 to 1.8 billion barrels. The former West Germany used 832 million barrels in 1989; Italy, 708 million barrels; France, 677 million barrels; and Britain, 634 million barrels. According to a *Global 2000* study, the developed countries of the world, excluding the United States, import 34 million barrels of oil per day while producing 18 million barrels.[76] Centrally planned economies have been less dependent on imports. The developing countries import 4 million barrels per day while producing 8 million barrels. In 1988, Third World countries imported oil at the following rates: Brazil, 217 million barrels per year; Chile, 28.5 million; Ghana, 7.1 million; India, 124 million; Ivory Coast, 6 million; Jamaica, 4.9 million; Kenya, 14.3 million; Pakistan, 27 million; the Philippines, 67.9 million; Senegal, 5.3 million; South Korea, 25 million; Sri Lanka, 13.3 million; Tanzania, 3.9 million; and Zambia, 4.2 million.[77] The significance of the imports, of course, depends on the size of the country and the effect of such importation on debt and debt service.

We are also depleting our supplies of natural gas. We have about the same amount of gas as of oil. At the rate we are using natural gas, we have about 120 years of it left.[78] It is frequently suggested that we can substitute natural gas for oil, even to fuel our cars. If we think of oil and gas as somewhat interchangeable, we would have about 90 years of supply at the present rate of use. Let me repeat: nobody thinks we will cut the use of oil and gas, despite rhetoric about how necessary such cuts are.

The fact is that we will soon deplete our supplies of gas if we continue to use them at the present rate. The supplies of gas are limited. We are living, for the most part, as if they were not. And, while estimates of the amount of reserves vary, the only significance of the variations is which of the next several generations will face the effects of oil and gas shortages—not whether such shortages will occur.

I take seriously the argument of the market economists who claim that there is a sense in which we will never run out of anything. If the market is allowed to function, we will keep increasing the price of a given resource as it gets in shorter and shorter supply, which will lead to changes in use patterns. So why all the fuss about the loss of nonrenewable minerals? Are there not always substitutable minerals? Will not the market take care of all these issues?

But if the market works as it seems to be working now, the use of nonrenewable resources without regard to their supply will throw us into actions such as the recent Gulf War to protect resources in short supply or to gain control of resources. If the pursuit of wood resources results in the destruction of tropical forests, thousands of species, and billions of tons of topsoil, are these losses not to be taken into account in some way? How does the market take into account the effects of market forces on persons who are not in a position to vote on market policies? How does the future affect the way we vote with our dollars?

It is useful to realize total U.S. energy in 1988 was provided by oil (42 percent), coal (24 percent), gas (22 percent), hydroelectric (4 percent), and nuclear (7 percent) power.[79] Estimates place total U.S. resources of coal at between 471 billion tons and 974 billion tons.[80] Estimates of U.S. consumption hover around 1 billion tons of domestic coal per year. At this rate of use, our reserves would last a good while. The U.S. consumption is about 4 tons per person per year.[81] If the population of the world doubles in the next forty years—which is certainly possible barring major increases in starvation—between 7 and 8 trillion tons of coal would be available for roughly 10 billion people. At 4 tons per person, there would be enough coal for a few hundred years.

Such speculation, of course, ignores the problem created by carbon dioxide emissions, which are expected to increase the average world temperature by 2.5 to 5.5 degrees centigrade in the next century. Any realistic assessment of this threat leads to the conclusion that either some way must be found to reduce the carbon dioxide emissions or to give up using coal and other fossil fuels. Coal is the worst offender, producing per unit of energy about twice as much carbon dioxide as natural gas and about 25 percent more than oil. One estimate has natural gas producing 70 percent more energy than coal for each unit of carbon dioxide emission. Various technologies have been developed for removing the carbon dioxide, but there is no solution that makes sense. For each ton of carbon (in coal and natural gas) burned, more than three and one-half tons of carbon dioxide are given off. To liquify and bury this carbon dioxide in the sea leaves us with the uncertainty of what happens when the containers disintegrate. To bury it in old gas wells is no more acceptable; we would have all the same problems faced with nuclear wastes, but with much more waste involved. The problem of acid rain due to the sulfur and nitrogen oxide emissions from burning coal probably *can* be solved satisfactorily with developing technologies—if we choose to use them. Thus, although we have a plentiful supply of coal for the future, the use of coal is very problematic.

There is little question that we need to reduce the amount of energy secured from fossil fuels and that we need to reduce the amount of energy demanded by our way of living.

Loss of Minerals—Nonfuels

The extensive consumption of nonfuel minerals accompanies the industrial revolution. According to a *Global 2000* study, six minerals are basic for modern life and international trade.[82] Estimates of the life expectancies of the supplies of these minerals differ, however. *Global 2000,* the U.S. Bureau of Mines, and the *Global Ecology Handbook* estimates, respectively, are as follows: bauxite (aluminum)—94, 248, and 50–100 years; copper—31, 67, and less than 50 years; iron—68, 212, and 100–200 years; phosphate—88, 255, and 50–100 years; potash—84, 610, and over 200 years; sulfur—26, 52, and no estimate.[83] Differences in these predictions may be explained by differences in the projection dates and in the rates of growth of use on which the estimates are based.

The *Global 2000* study also lists several minerals, presumably less vital, but still important. The projected estimates of the life expectancies of these minerals' supplies, by the three sources, are as follows: chromium—68, 703, and 100–200 years; industrial diamonds—8 years, no estimate, and no estimate; lead—29, 38, and less than 50 years; manganese—68, 414, and more than 200 years; mercury—21, 38, and less than 50 years; nickel—44, 131, and 50–100 years; silver—14 years, no estimate, and no estimate; tin—31, 12 years, and no estimate; tungsten—28 years, 63 years, and no estimate; zinc—21, 50, and less than 50 years.[84]

While there are some noticeable differences in the projections, there is considerable agreement that some important minerals are not going to last very long at present rates of use.

These studies do not take into account the possibility of using the oceans as sources for increasing the supplies of minerals. One analysis recognizes this potential with some estimates but notes that we are a long way from finding solutions to the political, economic, and environmental problems related to mining the oceans. Potential supplies of magnesium, aluminum, titanium, vanadium, manganese, iron, cobalt, nickel, copper, zinc, gallium, zincomium, molybdenum, and lead are large; in some cases, they are huge.

One other important aspect of mineral resources is the extent to which nations are dependent on other nations for supplies. The United States, for example, was dependent on imports (as of 1976) for the following percentages of its consumption totals: bauxite, 88 percent; chromium, 90 percent; copper, 16 percent; iron, 35 percent; lead, 12 percent; manganese, 100 percent; nickel, 61 percent; tin, 75 percent; and zinc, 60 percent.[85] Japan imported the same materials in the following percentages: bauxite, 100 percent; chromium, 95 percent; copper, 93 percent; iron, 99 percent; lead, 78 percent; manganese, 90 percent; nickel, 95 percent; tin, 90 percent; and zinc, 63 percent.[86] The European Economic Community imported these minerals in the following percentages: bauxite, 50 percent;

chromium, 95 percent; copper, 99 percent; iron, 85 percent; lead, 85 percent; manganese, 99 percent; nickel, 90 percent; tin, 90 percent; and zinc, 74 percent.[87]

In a nutshell, most countries of the world are dependent on stable world trade for the health of their economic systems.

Nonfuel mineral expenditures in 1976 were $200 per capita in the United States; $120 in Western Europe; $160 in other industrialized countries, including Australia, Canada, Japan, New Zealand, and South Africa; $30 in Latin America; $4 in Africa; and $8 in Asia and Oceania. For these same places, predictions for 2000 were $290, $180, $320, $40, $8, and $7. Obviously there are considerable differences in the population sizes of these areas.[88]

If all nations used as many minerals as the United States, the total expenditure for minerals would be $1.8 trillion, assuming an increase of 1 billion in the population.

It is worth noting that the less developed countries are in possession of considerable portions of the mineral reserves: iron, 36 percent; nickel, 55 percent; aluminum, 72 percent; copper, 48 percent; lead, 18 percent; zinc, 22 percent; tin, 83 percent; sulfur, 29 percent, and phosphate rock, 82 percent.[89] The significance of this for the politics of the world is considerable. If Third World nations could combine in some way, such as OPEC has at least been partially successful in doing, it could be an important factor in Third World economic development.

It is clear from this discussion of the way in which we are losing our life-support systems that a much more rational approach to the future is required unless we wish to face much more conflict and destruction of human life. How we can live with such increased conflict and destruction and still retain a measure of humanness and gentleness or a care for anything except survival is not clear. We seem to be racing toward catastrophes that stagger the imagination. We sometimes speak of a period in our history called the Dark Ages. We are headed for a tragic age, I believe, of a magnitude that is difficult to reconcile with anything we have been affirming for thousands of years about the nature of God and of humanity.

2

Why Our Social Institutions Are Not Responding Well to the Ecological Crisis

Economic Theory and Practice

Responses to the ecological crisis depend on one's determination of the source or sources responsible for the situation. The fundamental problems may be located in our technology, in our value systems, in the world views underlying our value systems, or in the economic and political systems that order our decision-making processes.

Some believe that the problem is primarily a technological one. For them, there is a technological fix. Change our technology, and the threats to our environment can be mitigated, if not overcome. Economic growth must be pursued in such a way that the growth can be sustained. Increased energy and water-use efficiency, sustainable sources for energy, and new technologies to reduce and treat wastes will reduce threats. Economic growth remains the goal. The ecological crisis, of course, is more than a technological problem because it involves the political and economic decision-making processes that determine which technologies will be developed and used.

Some feel that the threats to our environment are rooted in our value system, with its emphasis on the possession and consumption of things. This emphasis is based on a view of human nature as a bundle of insatiable wants without any limit except our capacity to satisfy them. There is no end, no contentment, no stopping place, nothing that is sufficient; there is no point where enough is enough. The self is thus viewed as an isolated self, externally related to others, created by its own choices. With such a value system, no amount of technological change will remove the causes of environmental destruction until we choose different lifestyles. Such lifestyle changes cannot be based on self-interest, say advocates of this view; any long-term approach to environmental problems must be based on a shift in the understanding of humans as internally related to each other, to nature, and to an underlying reality that holds the universe together.

Others claim that our addiction to things is due to our inability to handle the essential anxieties of death, guilt, and meaninglessness. This addiction pushes us into an endless round of activity. Such activity is in search of power, status, possessions, and money, the possession of which fills the holes in our lives, covering up the real self. Such a view assumes, of course, that there is such a "real" self. The root of the problem is the failure of our religions to provide acceptable, functioning solutions to the problems of death, guilt, and meaninglessness. In this understanding, no fundamental change will take place until convictions or circumstances drive us to a different view of reality and to religious and psychological therapies that free us from the addictions that dominate our lives.

At a deeper level, some see the fundamental issue as involving the whole Western mentality, with its focus on making, shaping, controlling, and creating reality. To be a creator or a cocreator of one's being leads to frenetic activity, to becoming, to never-ending external motion—whereas allowing one's being to emerge leads to internal motion, to an uncovering of what already exists. Such an uncovering of or connecting with being requires us to give up the purposes and goals our culture has conditioned us to pursue. The feminist critique of Western patriarchal culture has shown the way in which, without being aware of it, we can accept assumptions about reality for thousands of years without understanding that alternative decisions about what is real, true, or desirable can be made. What we are intended to be in our created being is much less clear today than it ever has been. What would provide deep satisfaction or fulfillment is much less understood and appreciated than most of us think. The ecological crisis suggests that we have been making some assumptions about what it means to be human and to be fulfilled that are very questionable. The physical, chemical, and biological world may be saying no at several different levels. This world may not be able to give us the content of the yes, but it certainly causes us to reexamine our yeses at all levels.

Another understanding of the human condition in our times roots the destructive environmental realities in economic theories and practices that do not take into account all the consequences of economic decisions and that are related to political institutions that are unable to provide a limit to the destructive consequences of their economic systems. In this section, I will focus chiefly, but not exclusively, on the reigning economic theory and practices in the United States.

Economic practice in the so-called market economies has produced a lot of material goods and services. The gross national products per capita are very high in the developed nations, which for the most part can be described as having market economies. Exceptions are, notably, the oil-rich countries of the Middle East. Some nations with market economies have done better than others in distributing resources to all their citizens. The United States, in which the market system has been followed in what might be called its purest form, has one-fifth of its population in poverty. But it has done well by the other 80 percent in terms of income that allows for the purchase of goods and services.

The United States, however, has done less well if the results of its economic practice are measured on the basis of other indices, such as damage to the biological basis for human life and to physical resources, or in terms of the socialization of human resources.

The United States produces about 18 percent of the total world carbon dioxide emissions and about 25 percent of the carbon dioxide emissions from fossil fuels. Insofar as carbon dioxide is said to be the chief gas responsible for global warming, our economic system must bear the responsibility for a large share of global warming. That is to say, our economic decisions result in the extensive use of fossil fuels, which emit huge amounts of carbon dioxide. In a similar vein, the destruction of the ozone, with the resulting increase in harmful ultraviolet rays, is a consequence of the functioning of the market, a market that in itself does not have a way of taking these consequences into account—except to pick up the pieces, to accommodate or adapt to the consequences. The market does not have a way of anticipating consequences. The market does not do much to prevent the loss of four billion tons of topsoil each year. The market does nothing to prevent the formation of acid rain; the destruction of forests, crops, ocean plants, and animal life; and the poisoning of water and food from pesticides and chemical fertilizers. So far as the market is concerned, we do what we can. The market results in our use of oil at rates that will deplete world resources in roughly 80 years and is sluggish in the development of alternatives (although Peugeot and Renault recently joined with the French government in a research project to develop hydrogen-fueled cars). Japan seems to have institutionalized nonmarket, government-supported and government-directed research that takes the future more into account than does the research conducted by U.S. industry, with its fear of anything except subsidies for what worldwide market institutions want. Allegedly, the U.S. government spent twenty-eight billion dollars accompanying oil tankers during the Iraq-Iran War to ensure that oil got to the refineries of the world's market economies, including our own. If we import somewhere around three billion barrels of oil in a year, that amounts to about nine dollars a barrel. These costs were not part of the market cost of oil. The same sort of subsidy is involved in the provision of federal dams and water for irrigation. Some 73 percent of the water available for drinking is said to be used for irrigation. Similarly, the cleanup of toxic wastes is not borne by the market operations; the U.S. government (and thus the U.S. taxpayer) has allocated nine billion dollars to clean up the worst toxic waste sites, with some estimating that it will take at least five hundred billion dollars to do the job.

It is claimed by those who defend the market system that all of these realities are external factors which the market system does not need to take into account. If they are externalities, the question is how to change the market system so that it anticipates consequences that threaten the very existence of human life. For example, market theory asserts that the way to handle the problems of poverty in developing countries—poverty that forces peasants not only to destroy tropical forests in search of land but also to grow crops for export to the neglect of food crops—is to encourage the poor to emigrate, legally or otherwise, to countries where there are more economic opportunities. Thus our southern border is a fortified zone to prevent illegal entrance. It is difficult to see how the new trade agreements and the flight of manufacturing from the United States to Mexico will respond to the great increase in population expected in Mexico and other south-of-the-border countries over the next forty years. As I have already pointed out, drastic measures in land redistribution and in the provision of health, birth control, and educational services are needed. The market does not make such provisions except slowly—much too slowly to prevent the mass emigration of poor persons from Mexico and other Central and South American nations to the United States.

Market advocates also claim that the externalities, insofar as they are perceived as threats, will be taken into account by our actions both in and outside the market. For example, once we are aware of the threat to our existence from global warming, we will stop using fossil fuels. Just how we can do this within the ten or twenty years that some claim we have before irreversible trends develop is not clear. But there is enough truth to this position to warrant our responsibility individually for some rather drastic changes in our lifestyles.

The fact is that in a society with a market economy and a democratic polity we do not have any way to conceive and implement the kind of changes that are required. For example, a recent poll showed that only about 10 percent of U.S. citizens would favor a twenty-five-cent tax on gasoline, a seemingly small price to pay to help clean the air. Few experts believe that such a small tax would cause the kind of dramatic change in the use of oil that is required, both from the viewpoint of decreased carbon dioxide emissions and because we only have somewhere between 40 and 60 years of domestic oil left at the rate we are using it.

The practical implications of market economics is even more evident when we examine the theory behind this practice. Market economics rests on the theory that decisions should be made by individuals and corporate entities. Underlying this theory is a view of reality which sees individuals as bundles of more or less insatiable wants. In seeking to realize what we want, we make more or less rational decisions about what we will give up for the sake of getting something we want. Some of us may want certain things for our children and grandchildren, but for the most part even what we want for them is determined by what we want for ourselves, without much regard for what other people want or what people might want fifty years from now. In this view, we will be able to continue our lifestyle for the next fifty or sixty years, so why worry about possible consequences, particularly when the myth under which we operate ensures us that the future will take care of itself. We are clever, and ways will be found—just as they have been found in the past to adjust to new problems, diseases, shortages, and temporary deprivations. Things will get better and better. More and more goods will be produced. The problems encountered by governments trying to systematically limit or shape economic growth are demonstrated by the recent failures of the centralized governments in Eastern Europe. It is a fact, of course, that environmental conditions are worse or no better in the former centrally planned economies than in the market economies. For years, the former USSR emitted almost as much carbon dioxide as the United States.

The fundamental theory underlying market economics is that the interaction of self-initiations is the only rational way to organize economic life. Economic institutions should maximize the freedom of the individual to initiate activity. For example, education, which in many ways chiefly prepares students to participate in economic life, should be left to the choices of individual parents and students. Parents should be given vouchers, which they can use at any of a number of schools on the basis of whether or not the school meets the criteria of the parents and the student.

Market theory, if fully implemented, means that the world becomes the market. Economic activities are carried out wherever the marginal cost for the last unit of anything that is made is the lowest. This means that investors and entrepreneurs will invest money in enterprises where the costs of production are the lowest and the profits, at least in the beginning, are high. Thus, in the present world market, manufacturing will take place in countries where labor costs are low—wages being low and benefits nonexistent—and restraints on pollution are least stringent. It is assumed, in part rightly, that restraints on wastes and emissions into the atmosphere increase costs. (Research has shown, however, that in some cases waste disposal reduction processes can save money for companies.) There is already evidence that American investment capital is moving to other countries. Mexican laborers earning two or three dollars an hour can be trained to do what American laborers demand much more per hour to do. Daly and Cobb claim in *For the Common Good* that this will lead to reduced wages and benefits for laborers in the United States.[1]

This scenario implies that more and more of American life will be disrupted as corporations move out. According to the market theory, labor will follow capital when and if the situation gets bad enough here, so U.S. workers can be expected to move to areas or even other countries where jobs are available for better wages. One of the arguments for such a world market is that developing nations will be helped by the jobs that are provided. In part this is true. But the kind of industry that is developed will provide export products and will not significantly aid in the development of a basic agricultural sector that can provide food. In some developing nations, millions of persons are literally starving to death because most of the economic attention is given to the development of export crops and products. What monies are available for development go for the infrastructure that supports export enterprises and not survival enterprises.

The same principle that applies to developing nations applies to the United States. Instead of funneling money into local and regional communities, the market encourages investment in new industries that destroy community roots by treating workers like abstract functions in an economy that moves them about or in and out of a job at will.

In market theory, nothing is sacred. There is no such thing as the common good. In a market economy, if there are structures and realities that establish limits and frameworks for good action, our temptations to ignore them are so great that no one can be counted on to act on anything except her or his own interest. We cannot count on others to act on our behalf. Therefore, we had better retain as much control of life as we can and only surrender in the face of being outvoted with other people's dollars or ballots.

Given the assumptions, theory, and practice of our present market system, what can we do? To start, we can work to change this system on all three levels.

If we attack the assumptions of market economics, we are raising what I would call the religious issues, not only in form but in substance. To believe, as I do, that there are given, created structures of life that set limits and provide the created opportunities for significant life means that we must raise fundamental questions about the reigning notion of freedom in Western culture. Freedom as self-initiation, as the power and the opportunity to be the cause of one's own motion, is the basic notion behind market theory and simple democracy. But to believe that one is only really free if one chooses that which contributes to the sustainability of the whole of the creation means that one must seek to discover and to formulate the content of freedom. There is no such thing as meaningful freedom unless one acts to support the biological basis for life. Hence, we must reject the present frenetic race to increase the production of things and the provision of services that threaten the future of the ecosphere. We must reject much if not most of what we are about. To prepare young persons for roles in our destructive economic system is not a meaningful calling. The first step is to say no to the present economic and cultural system and to participate in it as little as possible while waiting, seeking, praying, and hoping for another sustainable, fruitful, meaningful way of being. It is an active waiting, with expectation.

The second step is to rethink the theory of our economic system, attempting to think of economic practice within the context of the rest of life, rather than as an abstraction from the natural world. This is not a simple task. Economics courses might be taught as part of a course of study in which biologists, sociologists, theologians, as well as economists teach together. The basic question is, how can we think about the provision of goods and services in such a way that their production serves to sustain the biological basis for human life, maximizes human satisfaction in the production process, and takes into account the death every day of 40,000 kids under the age of five and perhaps another 130,000 adults from hunger and hunger-related diseases? Economic theory must provide a functioning system that does this. Herman Daly and John Cobb, in *For The Common*

Good, have tried such a theory. It is extremely important that such a theory deals with the challenges of both ecological destruction and poverty. Whatever withdrawal from the world market is involved should take into account the interconnectedness of the world on the ecological and human levels. The fundamental issue, I believe, lies in whether or not the economic system takes responsibility for the way it affects the whole of the creation. It is my conviction that neither a system that depends completely on self-initiations (market mechanism) nor a system that depends simply on rational choices by organizing centers (government agencies) is adequate. Rational persons of modest good will must be involved in decisions that are regulated in various degrees by the mechanisms of the market and of a democratic polity. The best institutions of all kinds, at all levels, will be shaped by a mixture of aristocratic and democratic forces, forces in which persons trained and socialized to focus on the common good will be balanced by others that are subject to some control by broadly based forces that also, hopefully, are somewhat focused on the common good.

We should build economic practice on the following principles. First, we should develop relative self-sufficiency at the lowest possible level. We should seek relative national self-sufficiency, relative regional self-sufficiency, and relative community self-sufficiency. National self-sufficiency implies, for example, that tariffs are used to prevent the flooding of the U.S. market by goods manufactured with our know-how and capital in other nations.

Second, we should seek resource provision within these self-sufficient areas where possible without excessive costs—a figure not easy to determine, of course. But there will be movement toward smaller-scale energy sources and smaller-scale food sources. National policy must set such developments as goals, and all programs for energy, water, farm, and tax policy should take these goals into account.

Third, economic activity should take place in such a way that more control can be exerted by the consumers over the conditions of production. This is particularly important in the area of food production, where there must be a reduction in the use of chemical fertilizers and pesticides. In all of this, the movement is toward participation in the production processes. More of the economic life must be of such a scale that consumers can effectively control the quality and the destructive effects of manufacturing.

Fourth, the economic system must be measured by indices that include the costs to individuals who are part of the system. To what extent does the system lead to poverty, racism, unemployment, low status for women, resource depletion, infant mortality and low birth weights, costs of transportation, accidents, pollution, the loss of wetlands, the loss of farmland and topsoil, the loss of species, crime, alcoholism, drug use, and other additions?

Fifth, we must find an optimum scale. How much pollution, how much waste disposal, how much carbon dioxide, how much methane, how many persons, how much species extinction, how much destruction of the wilderness, and how much mineral depletion can our biosphere and our society absorb? How much can humankind live with and without? How do we get scale considered on a national basis? On a global basis? How much can one society produce and consume without making it impossible for others to produce and consume even minimal amounts of the things needed for health and well-being? How does the scale of the present system effect the scales of future systems? What can be sustained over generations?

Sixth, assuming that relationships of some longevity and of some mutuality are important for human living, how does the economic system function to sustain them? How much fragmentation, mobility, impersonality, and lack of community can a society absorb without increased human and institutional pathologies?

These considerations point to several appropriate actions. For one, we need to participate in groups that listen to what the creation is saying to us and that seek to act on behalf of a sustainable way of life that does justice to the creation, seen both as a cradle for our lives and as having some intrinsic worth in the sight of God. Beauty is beauty. These groups can focus on education, on listening to what the natural world is telling us, and on what individuals as individuals can do in their own lives, in their families, and in their institutions to respond to the ecological crisis. Also, they can become part of or related to organizations that have economic pressure and political action as goals. It is important to organize these forces into local, regional, and national coalitions that function in relation to political parties and as economic forces to bring about change in our government and in our economic institutions. I have in mind something like Jesse Jackson's Operation PUSH and the Rainbow Coalition, which helped to bring about affirmative action. Such a movement would, in the first place, organize consumers to use their purchasing dollars to bring about changes in the behavior of economic institutions. These Green committees of correspondence might organize such action as well as political action that moves in the direction of the Green parties in other countries.

All of these responses to the ecological challenge can be called rational activity with somewhat observable and measurable goals and strategies. In addition, there is a role for what the Swiss theologian Emil Brunner labeled as eschatological action, action that is based on an assumption about how the world should be and might be when God's intentions for the creation come into being—a difficult assumption to make because no one can predict what is possible with God. Such action is also suggested by Rudolph Bahro, a German leader in thinking about these issues. The Cerro Gordo community of Cottage Grove, Oregon, was conceived as a model community to show some of the results of eschatological action. The goal is to organize some prototype communities of about twenty-five hundred people, relatively self-sufficient, whose way of being or lifestyle could be the basis for life everywhere—for all the predicted ten billion people of the world—without threatening the physical, chemical, or biological basis for life.

Educational Theory and Practice

The family, the school, and the churches and synagogues are the vehicles by which young people are supposed to be socialized. That is, in these institutions they are introduced to a way of being that is meant to realize their human potential in a way that holds the society together. Some contend that television is more effective than any of these. Depending on the perspective, the way of being taught by these institutions can be focused on the isolated individual, the society (usually the nation), the human race, or the whole universe.

Historically, there are four main starting points for teaching a particular way of being. First, there are those who focus on the whole universe, with a notion that there is something intentional about the universe as a whole, some direction in its development, and some given structure that sets limits and provides direction for human life. This structure may be referred to as God, as being itself or being in its depths, or as the genetic coding present from the beginning, from the first big bang. If we live in relation to this reality, there is fulfillment for ourselves and for the other reality. If we deny it and work in other directions, we destroy ourselves and the other reality. Humans, with their freedom, must make judgments about the content of that underlying reality and about what will actualize the potentialities present in it.

Second, there are those whose basic framework for life is provided by the society in which they are a part. This dominant way of being in a particular society (frequently thought of in terms of a nation state, although less and less so in modern times) is often referred to as the social system. Thus, the current tension in the Middle East can be understood as the clash of two different social systems, two different ways of being, two different founding myths, and two different sets of values—the Islamic tradition and the Western, more or less Judeo-Christian tradition, represented by Israel.

Whether or not the basis for each social system is founded on belief structures rooted in a more universal viewpoint is not always clear. Sometimes yes and sometimes no. But what more or less clearly dominates education is the preparation to participate in the functioning social system. The economic, political, military, and religious institutions provide the framework within which education takes place. Here and there, deviant educational opportunities are provided, with alternative interpretations of the meaning of life. Certainly in the United States, with its public education, there is an effort to prepare persons to fit into the functioning institutions. Theoretically, education is value free; that is, the teacher is not supposed to teach values or fundamental ideas about the meaning of life, at least not from the teacher's perspective. Teachers are to remain neutral in the great debates about the meaning of life and about the institutions that are desirable—unless they claim to have an objective, scientific point of view. Then, in the name of science, much is taught that by implication, at least, involves decisions about the ultimate questions. The point of this view of reality is to achieve a kind of neutrality on many issues and focus on so-called technical education. Technical education provides students with means, not ends, it is claimed.

It is true that within this framework, there is some emphasis on the humanities, namely, on the way in which historically different peoples have found different ways of looking at the ultimate questions. But even the humanities are taught with "objectivity," at least in theory.

This second point of view begins with the phenomena of the society, its institutions and the reigning cultural values explicit or implicit in those institutions. For this point of view, there is no other place to begin. The East-West debate has made it obvious, I think, that there is no real agreement on the nature of the institutions. The lull in the debate about capitalism and socialism, for example, is temporary. The debate is part of the inevitable dialectic, I believe, between self-initiation and other-initiation as useful tools for social organization. Both ignore the question about what such initiation is for, which to my mind is the most important question.

Education, in any case, is education to prepare one to succeed in the institutions of the particular society. It is more than technical, although it tends to focus on the technical. In our society, it includes a strong emphasis on competition to prepare students for a competitive, hierarchically organized society in which one moves into significant roles by virtue of certain competencies and by virtue of an aggressive, self-confident personality. One person describes this socialization process as preparing students for a win-lose orientation in life. Some win—some end up with the money and the power and the status—while others lose, getting very little of any of these goodies. In such a struggle, where there is room at the top for only a few, it is important to be trained away from any involvement with other persons. In such a system, one must be neutral, one must have the ability to put on blinders to the effects of one's actions on other people or on nature, and one must be free from involvements that take one away from concentration on the primarily technical tasks one performs. This is a required stance, even in the professions that deal with the inner lives of persons.

A third starting point for education begins with the individual, theoretically not socialized to anything in particular, but with certain nascent wants. This free-wheeling individual may accidentally bring along with his or her being certain values and certain desires, but these values are not grounded in any societal needs or values or rooted in some view of what an individual is meant to be, either alone or in relation to the whole. The notion that there could be some "intention" for the individual or for the whole of humanity is discarded. Such a notion has no meaning for persons who begin with the given individual in any state or condition that the individual happens to be in. Persons are what they are, and the only function of the society or of anybody else in relation to them is to provide a framework in which they can best "be what they want to be," whatever that is and whatever the consequences are—as long as they do not interfere too much with what someone else wants to be. Education, then, might be identified with what has been called permissive education. Such education provides permission for people to actualize whatever they happen to want to actualize; one simply takes a survey to determine what most people want.

A fourth starting point for education is the individual conceived of as having certain innate potentialities, the actualization of which leads to some sort of satisfaction or fulfillment that can be measured or identified in some way. In contrast to the third way of beginning (that is, beginning with an individual's felt wants or needs), this way asserts that the individual's needs may well lead to the destruction of a satisfying life, such destruction being defined by certain inabilities to function within certain institutions. The complexity of making such judgments is obvious—especially given the contention that it is a "real" sign of health today to be maladjusted to our present institutions. Who is maladjusted (and thus "sick") and who is adjusted (and thus "well") may not be obvious. Some recent psychological analyses begin with the hypothesis that it is possible to describe a healthy individual and then to look at both individual and collective behavior in the light of its contribution to the development of such an individual. These developmental approaches certainly have shed some light on the stages of healthy development. Education in this perspective involves being helped through these necessary stages and to an understanding of what makes for a fulfilled life—which may or may not involve historical judgments, as in the first and second perspectives. If an individual can be described as fulfilled or healthy without much regard for the fulfillment of a whole society in a particular period of history, then one can view the educational process for the individual in isolation from the world as a whole. This viewpoint is much different from one that sees all individual fulfillment in the context of universal fulfillment, in the context of what is best for the whole of society, the whole of humanity, and the whole of the natural world.

However, even though one begins with a notion of what an individual is meant to be, one cannot completely escape taking into account the realities of the given world, the context for the individual becoming fully developed. Thus, one must take into account what the society is like (the second starting point) or what the whole society is meant to be (the first starting point).

How then will the ecological crisis be addressed by the educational systems based on the four perspectives just discussed?

If we begin with the assumption that human desires are the focus for thinking about everything, the ecological crisis can be treated as a problem to be solved technically and politically. Thus we will make certain technical adjustments to accommodate the increasing toxicity as it affects those who are in power, or we will make political adjustments, such as the recent Gulf War, to ensure that there will be sufficient supplies of critical materials. We will also ask whether or not the values of our society are the cause of such havoc. We may have to treat the world as one society, given the effects of ozone-depleting and greenhouse gases on the whole world. Hence, some accommodations to the situations of other nations may be involved. That is to say, we may begin to treat the whole world as one society, in which case we must take seriously the values of other cultures and begin to use our educational system to understand how to deal with them.

However, these other parts of the world will be treated instrumentally—as something necessary to control or adjust to—and not as something in themselves calling on us to be different from what we as individuals want to be.

If we begin with the assumption that the values of our society are the determining values for ourselves (and thus with the assumption that they are the only useful values for the whole of the civilized world), we will function more or less as just described in relation to the rest of the world. Societal values are, after all, largely the result of the felt wants of individuals, freed for the most part from historical cultural factors that direct us in our search for fulfillment.

However, insofar as we do become more rational and recognize the instrumental relationships between at least parts of the world, the formation of a world society will begin, with demands recognized as part of the fact that we are dependent on each other for dealing with such matters as global warming, acid rain, and ozone depletion. This may, in time, lead to education that acquaints us with the nature of this interdependence and the requirements for taking it into account. Education will then have a component that prepares an individual to function within the world system as well as the national system. It still will be shaped generally by a pragmatic assessment of the extent to which either the individual's or the national social system's demands require adaptation to the demands of other social systems. The demands of the other social systems become instrumental demands, not intrinsic (that is, not due to the assumed demands of an essential individual or collective reality that requires certain kinds of responses if it is taken seriously). On the other hand, if one takes the position that there *is* an intrinsic state of being in which what happens to us happens to others and what happens to others happens to us, we will feel called on not to dump our toxic wastes wherever we can in the developing nations. In our enterprises, we will feel called on to exercise the same care with wastes in other countries as we would if we were dumping them in our own backyards. We might even go so far as to consider the forests and rivers and mountains as having a certain intrinsic value in the universe apart from their usefulness to us industrially or aesthetically.

Education can therefore be thought of as having similar content for different reasons or different content because of different assumptions about the nature of the world and of humanity. That is to say, everyone may see the possibility of global warming and include some information about it in their curriculum, but how that information is dealt with would be quite different. In one case, the concern could be within the context of a particular person's location and the effects on a personal or family business. Thus one would probably not invest in beach property at this time in history, especially where the sea-level rise is expected to wipe it out. One would begin to raise the dikes if one were in Holland. One would not invest in property in warm climates if one did not want to live where it is likely to be unbearably warmer. One might invest in land in some of the more temperate areas, where water supplies are not expected to be drastically affected. One might well orient one's existence toward activities that do not depend on climate stability for a steady income. One would tend to think of education as a preparation for accommodation. In the context of asking questions about use of energy, one might ask about energy efficiency or about renewable resources. But, if history is any indication of what will happen, interest in such projects will be based on simply continuing the lifestyle to which one has been accustomed. The threat of global warming is not sufficiently real in the short run or sufficiently personal for most persons to cause much action. The only perspective that seems to embody within its framework a concern for what happens to all persons living now and in the future is one that understands all being as interconnected.

If one took the position that all persons and things are connected, one would be much more concerned with curtailing the emission of global-warming gases. One might even press the analysis to ask questions about the values of a society that requires so much energy to exist. All this could take place in the context of the schools.

Some claim that modern science is discovering "empirically" that all the world is interconnected. All the realities of the heavens are moving away from us at a speed proportional to the distance from us such that one can infer that at one time they all started from the same point. Hence, everything began at the same place, as part of the same reality. In addition, scientists claim that this original reality always had the same dimensions that reality in its most developed form has today. They also claim that what happens to anything in some way happens to everything, that the communication among parts of reality is much more complex than we once thought. It is frequently affirmed, on this basis, that reality is not a group of isolated individuals, molecules, or atoms, externally related. Internal relations of a complex nature are present. From this point of view, science supports the first starting point to education—a focus on the whole universe—and education must tell this story in as much detail as possible. Education must include a consideration of the interconnectedness of all reality and hence the interconnectedness of the academic disciplines, disciplines that are now, for the most part, taught as if they can be dealt with in isolation from each other. Most technical education (viewed as a means with no particular end) would then be suspect because it would be assumed that there is no such thing as means without an end. The character of the means implies a certain end or purpose served by or implied by the means.

From this point of view, values are not merely subjective. They are part and parcel of a reality discerned by a careful examination of the world.

The myths and stories that portray a reality that leads to life must then be learned, and the interpretations of history when viewed from the point of view of an underlying structure of being must be worked out and shared. This is not to say that there will not be differences in opinion; however, we must reject the notion that one can get an education without being called on to locate oneself in the story of the universe. Teachers should be expected to articulate a coherent picture of the whole of humanity and nature.

If one assumes that the whole universe is an interconnected reality and that the enhancement of these connections is the purpose of one's life, then the production and possession of things will assume a subordinate place in the human enterprise. The real question will be whether or not one is united with reality in such a way that one supports and sustains other reality. Even knowledge will be understood as participation in other reality and can only be adequate if this participation precedes any attempt to articulate what it is that one knows.

The basic assumption of this analysis of education is that the present focus of Western culture on the production of massive quantities of material goods is no longer desirable. Therefore, the least that one can say is that an educational system preparing persons to participate in the production of the present material orgy is dysfunctional. To be a teacher and buy into most educational programs is to sell one's students short. The real question is how to share one's ambiguity about the present situation with students without cutting them off from the little meaning that is present in many of their lives. The only alternative is to begin oneself to live toward the future and to fashion one's classes to deal with how there can be a tolerable future for everybody. That means fashioning a future for the ten billion persons who will be living in the world by the year 2050. To think this way, I believe, will give a new content to education, an education that fits persons to be relevant to a future for everybody.

We are told every day to live one day at a time, and that may be what some persons must do. But the majority of persons need to begin to live with a vision of the future. We can be relevant only if we make a judgment about what that future should be like and then live accordingly.

My own preference wavers between thinking of education in the context of relatively small, self-sufficient communities (described in Chapter 4) and using education to help prevent the worst of the anticipated ecological disasters. We do need experiments with lifestyles that can be universalized, a movement much like the monasteries of the Middle Ages in which life was lived differently for the sake of humanity. In the present case, we would be experimenting for the sake of humanity and the natural world, the cradle of humanity.

Sometimes I think we need to be reborn into a way of thinking and being that focuses on the whole creation. I know that it is impossible to focus completely on the whole. We can only focus by attending to something in particular. But to place the particularities of our being and acting in the context of the whole creation is to change completely the reigning image of how life is thought about in our society—namely, the belief that by focusing on the part the whole will be served. It just is not true enough for me to take this claim seriously any longer. I know that there is some truth to it, but not enough. This point of view is responsible in large part for the trouble we are in. It may stem from the point of view of Thomas Hobbes, for whom life in the natural state, the state of nature, was the war of all against all. Or it may stem from the point of view of those who, while they affirm the existence of the whole—of God—feel that humans are so separated from God and each other that they are unable or unwilling to live in a way that takes the whole and others into account.

The results of this viewpoint are plain for us to see: increasing individual and social pathology and more destruction of nature. In a recent book, Theodore Roszak describes our situation as that of an endemic psychosis stemming from our denial of any ethical responsibility for our planetary home.[2] The solution suggested by Hobbes is a strong ruler who enforces cooperation. The market solution—the interaction of self-initiations on behalf of selves—is another way of handling the issue. As we have discussed, however, the market solution leads to a system in which the results of action are measured chiefly in terms of consumption and productivity because that is what most individuals want. There is probably not much that we can do to change this situation institutionally, given the entrenched belief in the market system in universities and powerful political institutions. Therefore, we probably have to move toward home education or the creation of communities with their own educational institutions. This probably will not make a lot of difference in the short run, but if things are as they appear to me to be, the long run will produce disasters in our society of such unimaginable magnitude that changes will be desired. In the meantime, we might learn what is possible. The most important thing, I believe, in thinking about education is to focus on the substance and avoid getting bogged down in arguing about symbols, important as symbols are to carry meanings. Thus, if the people involved in creation spirituality are describing the reality that I believe is represented by using some Christian symbols, I am not going to insist on using my symbols. For me, to be part of the body of Christ is to be connected with everybody and everything such that what happens to most anybody or anything happens to me, and vice versa. The connectedness is the important thing, not that we call it the body of Christ. But I will continue to call it that in my own thoughts.

Political Theory and Practice

Underlying the ecological crisis are economic, cultural, and political institutions that not only contribute to the development of the crisis but also lack mechanisms that allow for an intelligent response. In short, our political institutions do not have the self-correcting mechanism for responding to the situation.

I have already analyzed the way in which our economic and educational institutions contribute to the crisis. In this section, I will discuss how political institutions are based on theories and embody practices that are incapable of adequate response to the environmental revolution.

The theory underlying the political institutions of the United States is very much like the theory underlying the economic institutions. In this theory, the control of human behavior, insofar as it is social, involves the interactions of self-initiations. The basic agent of action is the individual. The agency (the initiator of action) is the interest of the individual. In economics, this is complicated by the interests of corporations. The fact that corporations follow their interests is justified by the assumption that corporations can only serve their interests by serving the interests of the consumers of their products and services. In political life, the individual voter is the decision-making agent. All decisions ultimately must be approved by voters, who either do or do not return legislators to office.

In our discussion of economic life and the environment, we saw that, in general, economic institutions do not take into account the effects of economic activity on the environment unless the government intervenes to assign costs for environmental degradation. Taxes or fines are assessed on the basis of rules and regulations established by governmental agencies. The costs for clearing up toxic wastes are forced on those responsible for causing the wastes, if guilt can be determined, or these costs are assumed by the government and borne by the general public.

Formulating regulations and assigning costs to economic institutions involves a political process in which the representatives of the people agree with the principle of governmental regulation and with the specific regulations. Regulation is opposed by most economic institutions in principle and in practice, except occasionally when it serves their interests.

The education and organization involved in pushing for minimal intervention in the marketplace involves considerable effort and resources ordinarily not in the hands of anyone except those who oppose such intervention. In this regard, the United States is one of the weakest nations in the world. Our general faith in market mechanisms and in a kind of simple democracy work against the kind of leadership required to deal with the ecological crisis.

For example, from any rational point of view, a long-term energy-efficient program for the use of fossil fuels should have led decades ago to rewards for energy efficiency to help reduce our dependency on foreign oil. Especially since the energy crisis in the early seventies, one would have expected national leadership to favor anything to reduce our dependency on and thus need to protect the supply of Middle Eastern oil. A rational policy would have worked to benefit our balance-of-trade deficits and to reduce our political commitments to keep the oil flowing. There is no indication that we have learned any lesson from the Gulf War. The billions of dollars involved in keeping the oil flowing, even before the war, should be added to the cost of every gallon of gasoline to understand its true cost.

The effort to change the political reality that continues to support policies avoiding a rational national energy program to reduce the use of oil, coal, and natural gas—thus reducing the threat of global warming and air and water pollution—has been absent. In spite of huge negative balances in trade payments, we are slow to require or entice our transportation sector and other oil users to become more efficient. Congressional action to increase the efficiency of our new cars is stymied by filibusters, lobbying, and a lack of any leadership from the executive branch. We are slow even to use market mechanisms to foster the efficiency of transportation. Imposing taxes comparable to those in western European countries is not supported by our leadership or by the citizenry.

In our kind of democracy, the people are expected to have an understanding of what is at stake and a concern for their own long-term interests and those of future generations. In fact, our political institutions and the ethos of our population generally do not allow either for an understanding of or a concern for the future.

Thus, one is led to the conclusion that the ecological crisis presents us with a political crisis. It is a crisis of such magnitude that in spite of the euphoria over the demise of the Eastern European centralized forms of government, the principle of intervention in the means of production needs to be reinstated without necessarily involving state ownership. There seems to be no way to move from the sense of triumph of the anti-intervention forces to a realistic assessment of what is required by the ecological crisis. The judgment that our institutions have the capacity to deal with all issues is a barrier to facing the present situation. It seems inconceivable to most economists and national leaders that the system that has brought us such prosperity can have any flaws. Fortunately, there are other countries in the same general political stream that have transcended the ideological stance of the market theorists and begun to move with some force toward programs that might save the world from seemingly inevitable disasters. There are also some U.S. political leaders who have a more advanced view of what is needed in the way of government action. Vice President Al Gore's book *Earth in the Balance* is an example of what I would call a balanced approach to the issues.

It is crucial to recognize that while Eastern European countries had the political instruments to deal with the environmental crisis, they did not move. In fact, those countries are ecological disasters. But to say that what has already happened represents disaster is to miss my point—we have not as yet begun to experience the most disastrous results of our productive enterprises on the life-support systems of the planet.

The fact is that neither our market system not the centrally organized systems of the remaining socialist countries have the understanding or the will to deal with the ecological crisis. The people who run both systems have such a stake in the short-term success of the present policies and corporate structures that they are blind to and uninterested in the effects on the future.

Both political systems are committed to lifestyles and to economic and political institutions that make it difficult for a rational, responsible program for a sustainable future to emerge. This is true even if one only thinks about the 5.3 billion persons in the world today; it is frighteningly true if one considers the predicted 10 billion persons by 2040.

Thus we are faced with a challenge for which our past politics are almost as inadequate as our past economics. It is crucial to avoid the trap of thinking that what worked in the past will work in the future. A simple question to ask oneself is, how will our political system arrive at the decisions and the actions needed to limit our carbon dioxide emissions to about 20 percent of what they are today in the next twenty years?

There is no easy way for our present political system to provide us with the kind of actions we need in economics, education, and every other aspect of our lives. We live with an uncertain future for which a new politics is needed. This new politics involves four elements. First, we need leadership, persons who combine a charismatic personality with a knowledge of the state of the world. Observers used to ask Teddy Roosevelt why it appeared that others always agreed with him. He answered that he simply made up his mind and then proceeded to persuade the people of the wisdom of his decision. We need some wise leaders who prefer truth and wisdom to the easy victories that come with promises of short-term benefits. Politics must become more than a popularity contest, with decisions made in response to the polls.

Second, we need a massive educational effort. Part of the job of political leadership is to educate the people. With communication systems providing access to millions of people, some way must be found to use these powerful tools for educational purposes, such as in the videotapes "After the Warming" and "Race to Save the Planet." A strategy must be worked out to develop spokespersons, access talk shows, and set up public debates.

Third, we need to fund and establish a center for strategic planning and for the education of the national leadership. This may be in the making with the commitment of three national foundations to a focus on energy. Somehow the interests of the Green committees of correspondence, the establishment-oriented operations, and the groups focusing on a creation-centered ethos must be combined. It would be a mistake, I believe, to avoid the conversations that must go on between those who think that there are technological solutions and those who think that the underlying premises of Western civilization are in question. Both directions, in my judgment, must be pursued at once. It is at this point that the churches have an opportunity to be useful in asking fundamental questions about the ethos of our present culture.

Fourth, we should develop a strategy for using the purchasing power of a growing number of environmentally conscious citizens. The experiences of the African American community in using its purchasing power to achieve some movement toward affirmative action suggests one approach. Corporate America can be persuaded to move toward environmentally responsible action—which is often in their best interest, even in the short-run—by organizing consumers to withhold their purchasing unless corporate policy begins to take the future of the environment into account. Jesse Jackson's Operation PUSH provides some basis for understanding how this can be brought about. My own seven-year experience with this organization suggests that it can be positive for everyone involved. Regardless of whether it is perceived as positive by corporate America, by government bureaucracies, or by consumers, we should attempt such action.

Unless we act politically to take the future into account, there will be no sustainable future for anyone.

The Ecological Crisis and the Misunderstanding of Freedom

The environmental movement raises a serious question about the notion of freedom that prevails in American society. In raising this question, it also raises questions about our understanding of ourselves and about the goals of a society based on such an idea of freedom.

According to this prevailing notion, to be free is to choose according to one's preferences. Society should thus be organized to maximize the opportunity for individuals and institutions to choose to do what they prefer to do. Choice involves internal principles. The less interference with choice, with self-initiation, the better. The chief limits, aside from a general framework of law and order, are imposed by the interactions of self-initiations. These interactions take the form of the marketplace and the freedoms of speech, assembly, and the press. With this understanding, the best governments are those that intervene least in setting limits on human action.

There is a contrary view that posits a conflict between freedom conceived as self-initiation and what might be called destiny—between doing as one pleases and taking into account certain structures of reality that set somewhat indefinite but real limits to what can be done without destructive consequences. Self-initiated freedom is distinguished from true freedom, which takes destiny into account. In this view, interference with self-initiation for the sake of taking the limits of reality into account are not in principle counterproductive.

Move too far in either direction, toward freedom as self-initiation or toward determinable boundaries or limits, and life becomes problematic. In this view, the socialist societies moved too far in the direction of setting limits on freedom of action, and the so-called free societies have moved too far in the direction of the freedom to act without taking the destructive consequences into account. The individual and social pathologies common in our cities as well as the environmental crisis point to the failure of our society. While the chaos of our cities and our environmental policy cannot be totally blamed on the principles of self-initiated freedom and its chief institutions (the market, democratic politics, and permissive education), these institutions cannot escape some responsibility for what is happening.

The environmental movement calls attention to the chemical, physical, and biological limits that, if ignored, could result in catastrophic costs. For example, the environmental movement contends that ozone filters out destructive ultraviolet rays in a way that prevents damage to plant life and to humans in the form of skin cancer, cataracts, and immune system problems. Human action that results in the destruction of ozone thus becomes questionable. The question is whether or not persons and institutions should be free to destroy ozone. A second question, of course, is, how should such action be eliminated? To what extent should freedom of self-initiation be limited? What are the proper mechanisms to implement such limits—education and voluntary action, citizen pressure, government regulation, or taxation? How can the actions of persons all over the world be limited? How can property rights and market mechanisms be used to take into account environmental degradation?

A second example, much more controversial, finds the environmental movement calling our attention to global warming. The global temperature-controlling gaseous blanket in the stratosphere is another given, structural limit or factor of destiny. It can be ignored only if the consequences of ignoring it are said to be irrelevant in the human decision-making processes. We can act as if we were free from its limitations, or we can find ways to take the possibility of dramatic climate changes into account. The environmentalists claim that we should not be as free to initiate what we please; the consequences of freedom seem difficult to justify simply to preserve the opportunity for persons to initiate whatever they prefer.

The issues are not new. The debate persists between those who assume that we are more or less isolated individuals whose interest is a "care for [our] own happiness, that of [our] family, [our] friends, [our] country"[3] and those who believe that we are more integrally related to and therefore interested in the results of any action for a whole range of reality, human and nonhuman. The environmentalists tend to come down on the side of intimate and integral connections to the universe. The debate involves, on the one hand, those who insist that what is important is the opportunity to initiate, to be the efficient cause of action, and to be limited only by other self-initiating human entities. Social interaction thus results in the just and efficient production of whatever initiators happen to prefer. On the other hand, there are those who believe that we must formulate views of what preferences are more desirable, more in tune with supporting and sustaining opportunities for all persons now and in the foreseeable future—that take destiny into account.

In purely formal terms, the issues revolve around those who focus on efficient and formal causation and those who focus on final and material causation. At one level, the issue is practical. Which principles for the organization of society will best lead to a fulfilling life for all humans and some sensitivity to the value and meaning of the nonhuman world beyond its instrumental use in the production of useful goods? It can be argued that the interaction of self-initiations, which I would accept as a valid regulating principle for society, is also the only available constituting principle for determining the ends for which society can be organized. At another level, I, with the deep ecologists, would argue that the destructive consequences of human activity are unlikely to be taken into account unless we have convictions about the way in which the fulfillment of any individual is related to the fulfillment of other individuals and the natural world.

I also suggest that those who focus on the market system of organizing preferences are likely to have convictions that ignore the various environmental crises, treating them either as unimportant externalities or arguing that they do not in fact constitute threats to life. Recently, I asked Kent Jeffreys, Director of Environmental Studies for the Competitive Enterprise Institute, what his principles implied for dealing with the ozone issue. His long response argued against the existence of ozone depletion as an issue; there is no significant ozone depletion, he said. He had argued in a previous formal presentation that one could expect the environmentalists to find reasons for governmental intervention, implying of course precisely what I am implying—that one's general presuppositions about life and one's theory of social action affect one's perceptions of the so-called facts. It is not surprising to find market advocates suggesting that we should dump our toxic wastes in developing countries because they would profit from the money earned. The benefits outweigh the costs, they claim, or at least equal them. Nor is it surprising to find such advocates saying that if persons must die from starvation, it is preferable that persons who earn little rather than persons who earn a great deal should die, if there is a choice. This way of thinking encourages viewing persons almost exclusively in terms of what they produce in the way of measurable products.

Likewise, I must hasten to say that it is not surprising to find advocates of social ownership and governmental intervention using the environmental movement to justify their support of such intervention to protect the environment.

The implications of my analysis can be found in a recent publication, *For the Common Good: Redirecting Our Economy toward Community, the Environment, and a Sustainable Future*. The authors, an economist and a theologian, begin, as I do, with an understanding of reality based on Alfred North Whitehead's philosophy that everything is related to everything else. Thus, the way in which any action supports, sustains, and in some sense becomes a part of other events and individuals is basic. Initiations that do not take such connections into account ignore part of what is real. The authors claim that much of our social philosophy, especially our economic theory, in principle ignores the social costs of using self-initiation and the interaction of self-initiations as the constituting reality for society. A symptom of this theory is a focus on the gross national product as the chief measure of economic welfare. These authors insist that we take into account the other results of the focus on self-initiations. Hence, their index of social welfare includes a consideration of income distribution, net capital growth, foreign versus domestic capital, natural resource depletion, environmental damage, the value of leisure, and the value of unpaid household labor. Their index of sustainable economic welfare contains twenty-five items, including the loss of farmlands, the loss of wetlands, the costs of noise pollution, the costs of air pollution, the expenditures for national advertising, the private and public expenditures for health and education, the maintenance of streets and highways, and the expenditures on consumer durables. All of this indicates a concern for the results of the system, results that move way beyond a simple monetary measure of production or income.

Hence, these authors move the discussion of the concept of freedom to new levels. They expose as inadequate the attempt to organize society around the freedom to self-initiate according to our preferences because such a mode of organization produces more total dollar income. This book (as well as many others—I especially call your attention to the publications of The Other Economic Summit/Americas[4]) demonstrates the important role that environmental considerations have played in raising questions about the reigning notion of freedom in our society.

3

Theological Foundations for Responding to the Ecological Crisis

The Bible as a Foundation

It is clear that we who claim to be rooted in the Christian tradition must listen more to what the world is telling us. The Bible tells us to listen to the creation, to what we call nature. In previous chapters, I have sought to support my conviction that the biological conditions for human life are threatened; we cannot sustain our present lifestyles. We must act as Christians and take responsibility for the results of our lifestyles. This presents us with a dilemma: we cannot be Christian in the modern world. The modern world and Christianity are contradictory. We cannot buy into the lifestyle of the modern world and still claim to be Christian. We have to give up our Christian faith or radically change almost everything we are and do. There is no way to justify what we are about from the viewpoint of the Christian faith. We stand under radical judgment.

For me, the Bible is the Word of God, but it is in no simple sense the Word of God. The eyes and ears and minds and hearts of those who experienced events and interpreted them as God's actions affected what we read in the Bible. Those who heard voices and interpreted them as God's voice or those who saw burning bushes that did not burn—they interpreted all of this as God speaking. They wrote something down or told stories that later were written down. Those who wrote the stories, those who copied what was written down—all are in some way prisms of the Word of

God. Somehow, we have to uncover the Word of God under these layers of subjectivity, under all of the personal histories of those whose words we now read. The words are not the Word of God, and yet they can become the Word of God for us. Furthermore, there is a history of listening to the Bible. Roman Catholics for instance, rely heavily on tradition, creeds, and encyclicals that are formally said to embody the Word of God. All of us have our traditions, our creeds, our catechisms, our rituals, our hymns, our favorite theologians. Ideally, when we take a passage or two each week as the basis for the proclamation of the Word—the sermon—the preacher and the congregation should listen to the great historical monuments of interpretation of the Christian faith: Augustine, Luther, Bultmann, Barth, Thomas, Calvin, Fox, Hall, Ruether, Soelle, Eisler, and so forth to sort out the layers of subjectivity, including our own, in listening to the words of the biblical writers.

Furthermore, the world of the preacher and of the listeners is changing. History turns up new situations, new realities, and the Word must address these new situations. The world is never quite the same.

Furthermore, a free God is not bound to the Bible, to the church, to the creeds, or to the traditions. There is a new Word for each situation, in some sense new and in some sense old. The problem is sorting out what is always the same and what is different. Even other traditions have something to say. I call myself a Jewish, Catholic, Protestant. I find in the Old Testament, the Jewish Scriptures, truths that speak to the human situation today; I find in the Catholic traditions some helpful words; and I am steeped in Protestant thought, in Luther, Calvin, Schleiermacher, Barth, Brunner, Reinhold Niebuhr, Richard Niebuhr, Bonhoeffer, Tillich, Hall, Brueggemann. Looking over this list, it is obvious that I have ignored the feminine voices in the church. Gandhi had somebody read to him every day for an hour from the Bible, especially from the New Testament, and from the Bhagavad Gita. He opened himself to hearing different sources of truth.

We also must hear the Word of God in the creation. In Rom. 1:18–20 we read the following:

> For the wrath of God is revealed from heaven against all ungodliness
> and wickedness of those who by their wickedness suppress the truth. For
> what can be known about God is plain to them, because God has
> shown it to them. Ever since the creation of the world his eternal power
> and divine nature, invisible though they be, have been understood and
> seen through the things he has made.

In the things that have been made, we can see, hear, and perceive the Word of God. For me, this means that we must look at the things that have been made. And we must look at what is going on in the things that have been made with all the help we can get. Many scientists are telling us that we are living in a world that is so connected, so interrelated, that we cannot act without affecting everyone else. They point to our use of coal, oil, and gas and to the by-product carbon dioxide, which forms a blanket around the earth and is warming the earth with, they say, disastrous consequences.

Now, we already really know this, for we have read in First Corinthians:

> Just as the body is one and has many members, and all the members of the body, though many, are one body, so it is with Christ. For by one Spirit we were all baptized into one body. . . . Indeed the body does not consist of one member but of many. If the foot would say, "Because I am not a hand, I do not belong to the body," that would not make it any less a part of the body. And if the ear would say, "Because I am not an eye I do not belong to the body," that would not make it any less a part of the body. If the whole body were an eye, where would the hearing be? If the whole body were hearing, where would the sense of smell be? But as it is, God arranged the members in the body, each one of them, as he chose. If all were a single member, where would the body be? As it is there are many members, yet one body. . . . God has so arranged the body . . . [that] the members may have the same care for one another. If one member suffers, all suffer together with it; if one member is honored, all rejoice together with it (12:12–20; 24–26).

Some say that this passage only applies to those baptized into the church. But then we read in the prologue to the Gospel of John: "In the beginning was the Word, and the Word was with God, and the Word was God. He was in the beginning with God. All things came into being through him, and without him not one thing came into being" (1:1–3). And in Colossians, we read: "He is the image of the invisible God, the first-born of all creation; for in him all things in heaven and on earth were created, things visible and invisible, whether thrones or dominions or rulers or powers—all things have been created through him and for him" (1:15–17).

Theologically speaking, the essence of Christ is the essence of the creation. The being of Christ gives us a picture of the being of the creation. Everything is connected with everything else, and to the extent that we are with Christ, we are with God and God is with us.

We are not isolated, externally connected individuals. We are internally related; everything that happens to me happens in a less important way to you, and vice versa. Everything that happens to the land happens to you and me. We are connected to the world, the biological and physical world surrounding us, undergirding us, in and through us. So God is saying something to us through nature. The Word of God is coming to us through nature, just as it came to the writers of the Old Testament through nature.

Listen to Jer. 3:1–5:

If a man divorces his wife and she goes from him and becomes another man's wife, will he return to her? Would not that land be greatly polluted? You have played the whore with many lovers; and would you return to me? says the Lord. Look up the bare heights, and see! Where have you not been lain with? By the waysides you have sat awaiting lovers like a nomad in the wilderness. You have polluted the land with your whoring and wickedness. Therefore the showers have been withheld, and the spring rain has not come.

Some of this is figurative (the whore, for example, represents anyone who has given up God). Simply put, the prophet here is saying that if we are unfaithful to God, nature responds. If we are unfaithful to each other, nature responds.

Now listen to Ezek. 33:23–29:

The word of the Lord came to me: Mortal, the inhabitants of these waste places in the land of Israel keep saying, "Abraham was only one man, yet he got possession of the land; but we are many; the land is surely given us to possess." Therefore say to them, Thus says the Lord God: You eat flesh with the blood, and lift up your eyes to your idols, and shed blood; shall you then possess the land? You depend on your swords, you commit abominations and each of you defiles his neighbor's wife; shall you then possess the land? Say this to them, Thus says the Lord God: As I live, surely those who are in the waste places shall fall by the sword; and those who are in the open field I will give to the wild animals to be devoured; and those who are in strongholds and in caves shall die by pestilence. And I will make the land a desolation and a waste, and its proud might shall come to an end; and the mountains of Israel shall be so desolate that no one will pass through. Then they shall know that I am the Lord, when I have made the land a desolation and a waste because of all their abominations that they have committed.

Walter Brueggeman asserts, in his book *The Land: Place as Gift, Promise, and Challenge in Biblical Faith,* that the land responds, or God uses the land to make a response, as is affirmed in these biblical passages. There is a connection between what we do and nature. In the things that God has created and in what happens to them we can perceive God speaking.

The book of Isaiah contains a reverse of the message in the Ezekiel passage just quoted. This is one of my favorite passages. Listen:

> *Ho, everyone who thirsts, come to the waters; and you that have no*
> *money, come, buy and eat! Come, buy wine and milk without money*
> *and without price. [This is grace, of course.] Why do you spend your*
> *money for that which is not bread, and your labor for that which does*
> *not satisfy? Listen carefully to me, and eat what is good, and delight*
> *yourself in rich food. Incline your ear, and come to me; listen, so that*
> *you may live. I will make with you an everlasting covenant, my*
> *steadfast, sure love for David. . . . For as the rain and the snow come*
> *down from heaven, and do not return there until they have watered the*
> *earth, making it bring forth and sprout, giving seed to the sower and*
> *bread to the eater, so shall my word be that goes out from my mouth; it*
> *shall not return to me empty, but it shall accomplish that which I*
> *purpose, and succeed in the thing for which I sent it (55:1–3; 10–11).*

Thus, if we listen carefully to the earth, it will sustain us.

Now, listen to this: "For you shall go out in joy, and be led back in peace, the mountains and the hills before you shall burst into song, and all the trees of the field shall clap their hands" (Isa. 55:12). When I am at Holden Village, I can understand this. The mountains and the hills before one do break forth into singing, and the trees clap their hands. "Instead of the thorn shall come up the myrtle; and it shall be to the Lord a memorial, for an everlasting sign which shall not be cut off" (Isa. 55:13).

Interconnections thus exist between persons and nature. There are interdependencies, causes and effects, responses, withdrawals, and affirmations between human and natural realities.

Finally, I want to affirm what God is doing in our time. As you read your newspaper, I ask you to remember Moses and Pharaoh. (I do this with my tongue in my cheek—but only partially in my cheek.) In Exod. 10:1–2 we read, "Then the Lord said to Moses: 'Go in to Pharaoh; for I have hardened his heart and the heart of his servants, that I may show these signs of mine among them, that you may know that I am the Lord.'" As I struggle to make sense out of what we are doing to the earth, the air, and ourselves, I am led to say that anyone who has been reading the newspapers knows that we are making a mess out of life. We read about unemployment at the top, middle, and bottom; school dropout rates as high as 50 percent; increases in suicides, homicides, rape, and child and woman abuse; drugs; poverty; stress on the job; mental illness; fraud; racial conflict; the selling of influence in high and low places; the manipulation of financial and commodity markets; the manipulation of corporate ownership; teenage parents; alcoholism; the wounded children of chemically dependent parents; death squads; automobile accidents with and without drunken drivers; violent conflicts here and abroad—to name only a few examples of this disintegration.

We also read of burying ourselves in garbage, which in turn pollutes our underground water. We read about the destruction of lakes, rivers, and oceans as habitats for life. We read about polluted air, polluted food, polluted drinking water, about ultraviolet rays that threaten our immune systems, about predictions of gigantic climatic changes, about dying forests, and about soils losing their fertility.

It is tempting to believe that God is finally saying no to our way of life. How long will we resist repenting and turning from our destructive ways of living?

When I listen to the earth, I hear God hardening the hearts of the dominant forces in our land to bring about such disaster that the bankruptcy of the American way of life—of the industrial culture of the modern world—will become clear to all who have eyes and hearts to perceive.

With those who repent and begin to turn from their idolatrous ways, God will form a covenant not to destroy the creation completely but to create a new community of faith and hope, a community with a new direction, a new vision.

It will be a community in which the whole earth and all its peoples will be cared for. A way quite different from the way that emphasizes possessions, things, bigness: big cars; big houses; big incomes; big positions in the economic, political, educational, social, and religious spheres; big names; big noise; big televisions; big productions; big farms; big yachts; big trips; big photo albums; big slide collections; big libraries; big, fancy celebrations; big power. *Big,* regardless of the consequences, is the watchword of our society.

It is only a question of time until this Tower of Babel comes tumbling down.

You may not hear what I hear. But I invite you to listen to what scientists are telling us. We need to listen to what nature is saying to us. Listen, listen, listen. There is only one way I know to listen, and that is to read the scientists' reports on what is happening and then visit the scenes of the degradation of our environment.

We have developed a way of life that destroys nature and, in principle, is not responsible for our neighbors near or far. We are convinced that we can worm or work our way out of every predicament with new technology, and thus remain as we are. But the land is the voice of God. What the land is declaring today is that something is radically wrong with our way of life. Nature is saying no to the Western world. That is the Word of God for today.

Let me close this section on a positive note. I do believe that this no can be a door to opportunity for those who are free from the demand to participate in our present system and to justify ourselves by what we earn—free to listen until something clear is heard about what is happening to nature and to us.

I am glad to be a senior, retired, without anything that I have to do to live modestly. And, before you remind me, I know that my modest living is dependent on the system that seems to me to be so idolatrous. For the time being, at least, I do have the freedom to listen and to think about being something other than what I have been. All of us have the freedom to be something different. God help us and our children and our grandchildren if we do not choose something different from what we have been. What an opportunity for new life!

Theology and Philosophy as Resources

To be in community is to be. All of us are ourselves to the extent that we are parts of each other and parts of the created world. We are in community both by virtue of recognizing and accepting our interconnectedness through God and the creation and by virtue of our experiencing each other and integrating that experience into our being. When we support, sustain, and enhance each other, we are in community.

Many years ago I learned from the philosophy of Alfred North Whitehead and Henry Nelson Wieman that to be is to be an individual in community. Charles Hartshorne developed the notion of the compound individual. In this view, we are at once individuals in community with each other and with God—and with the other parts of the creation. Any experience of persons or of truth or of beauty can be a building of the individual and an appropriation of other individuals and realities. In *Love, Power, and Justice,* Paul Tillich describes four types of love, four types of union with reality. *Libido* is union with reality of less being than oneself, such as food; *philia* is union with reality that is of equal being with oneself, such as friendship; *eros* is union with being that in some sense is of more being than oneself, such as truth and beauty; *agape* is union with other reality in spite of the state or condition of the other reality. We are ourselves insofar as we unite with being, or accept the given unions that underlie our existence.

There is, therefore, no way not to be in community or union with life; the question is how much individuality we have in community. For we are to the extent that we absorb and integrate other reality into our being; hence we are to the extent that we are in community. Four questions emerge for us in the modern world. Do we accept the fundamental created interrelationship or community as a given? Do we focus on setting up the conditions for the individual in community to grow, or do we focus on helping the individual to grow in a kind of isolation from the community? Do we need to establish communities in which there is a focus on the individual in community as over against the individual in isolation? Do these communities exist in the context of other interconnections given in creation, interconnections that tie us to all of humanity and to all of reality?

Several conceptual or analytical perspectives are useful to me in looking at the nature of reality: Paul Tillich's ontology, Richard McKeon's framework for looking at the history of thought, Talcott Parson's analyses of modern and traditional societies, and Saint Paul's organic metaphor of the body.

Paul Tillich's ontology pictures the world as two polar structures, one on the horizontal level and one, figuratively, in the vertical dimension or direction. On the first horizontal plane, all reality is a mixture of individualization and participation. To be is to be an individual center of acting, reacting, receiving, and shaping, in some sense a deciding center, although the meaning of this for an atom is different from what it is for a human being. At the same time, to be is to participate in being, in the physical world, in fields of force, in gravity, in communities and institutions. Tillich says that if you stay at home too much and build yourself up with all kinds of reflections and integrating activities (individualization), you destroy your self; likewise, if you go out too much and have all kinds of experience without taking time for integration (participation), you destroy your self. He also says that the unlearned artisan who asks significant questions about life can have more being than a professor who can tell you about what is in thousands of books, who knows a great deal about what other people think. What one brings to any inquiry or any experience makes a great deal of difference in the world. We shall return to this later when we consider the vertical dimension.

The second set of horizontal polarities involves dynamics and form. Life is a pulsing, throbbing bundle of energy, like the moving water of a lake or ocean. This more or less unformed energy pushes for expression in all kinds of ways at many different levels, physical, biological, social, and spiritual. It finds its expression in forms that limit its dynamism, give shape to its shapelessness. One can focus on the expression of a restless, surging, somewhat uncontrollable reality, or one can focus on forms, even to the extent of claiming that there are certain eternal forms, once and forever given as directions for the fulfillment of life. One can say that life is always meant to be embodied in certain forms or that all forms have a history. At certain times, some are more relevant than others for meeting the emerging history of humankind and of nature. Again, there is a dialectical relationship for Tillich. Sometimes forms need to be broken by the restless urging of a restless, almost formless energy (dynamics). At other times, it is crucial to surround the restless energy with forms that have been historically proven to have a particular relevance for particular situations.

The third set of horizontal polarities involve freedom and destiny. On the one hand, there is freedom, defined as self-initiation. This is freedom to be the first and initiating cause of any action in which one is involved. One is free to do as one pleases without restrictions, unless they are self-imposed. On the other hand, there are limits, directions, realities that are simply destiny. I used to say it is my destiny to be male, using whatever we could agree on to indicate what that means. Now I know that in our freedom we have discovered ways to overcome even this reality. I am white, and I was born in the United States. This is destiny. As you can see, however, these terms are slippery. Just how much freedom and how much destiny I have is never a matter of formula or past events. There are those, of course, who believe that their destiny is predetermined, foreordained, providential, and that their free choice has little or nothing to do with their future or the history of the world. Hence, in a strange reversal, they are free to do anything they please because their ultimate destiny is already determined.

An example of destiny is provided by the present ecological crisis. If, in our freedom, we have chosen to use chemicals that when released into the atmosphere destroy the ozone, we have defied destiny in our freedom but at the cost of an increasing number of cancer patients and early deaths. Similarly, if in our freedom we burn fossil fuels more or less without limit, we are placing a blanket of carbon dioxide around the earth that in due time will cause a change in our climate with all kinds of negative results— results due to our thwarting of a destiny that is defied or violated only at the cost of human life. Freedom and destiny exist in a dialectical relationship such that a balance must be reached in each historical period or in each decision for life to go on in a meaningful way—or to just go on. For example, some claim that the explosion of nuclear bombs will also release nitrogen oxide into the atmosphere at heights that will immediately destroy significant portions of the ozone.

In the vertical polarity of Tillich's ontology, we have the secular, profane, or one-dimensional world, and we have the holy, sacred, two-dimensional world. For me, and I believe for Tillich, whatever choices one makes on the horizontal dimensions, these choices are always made whether or not one is aware of it, in the context of a depth dimension. We are involved in the whole of existence, including a reality behind and around and underneath our ordinarily experienced world. God is in and through and around and underneath everything—much like, for comparison's sake, the field of gravitational force in which we exist.

God is free from absolute form for the realization of purposes in creation. Hence, a historical judgment is always required as to where we are in balancing the various dialectical relationships.

This leads me to set forth Richard McKeon's analysis of the alternative ways of looking at reality, upon which I have based my analysis of educational systems. Those who believe that the only real world is the world that is experienced, the so-called phenomenal world, may begin with the feeling, sensing, generally small and self-centered part of that world, the individual. Or they may begin with a given social system with certain values and preferences. The real is the phenomenal whole, the given whole. The responsible goal is to socialize everyone so that they can function within the system according to the system's norms and standards.

For McKeon, other positions affirm that there is either an essential individual or an essential whole. Some affirm that we have been created or exist with a kind of individual, essential nature. This nature is buried beneath all kinds of experiences, complexes, habits, and interpretations that prevent us from being the way we would be if we actualized potentialities that provide real, deep, lasting, fulfilling experiences. Through education, therapy, positive conditioning, and social structures, this deep self can be actualized.

McKeon also claims that there are those who see the world as existing with another world, a whole, behind the phenomenal world of ordinary experience. Often, some ritual, meditation, or "mountain-top" experience serves as a vehicle for us to reach through the layers of the phenomenal world to this deeper world. Whatever we are meant to be can never be known except in the context of this essential whole. Thus Aristotle, for example, discusses what is the good for the person as a person, as if there is a good for a person as an individual. He also discusses what is good for a person as a citizen, which requires actions not necessarily in harmony with what is good for a person as a person. In this way, the good of the whole stands above the good of the individual. Both are rooted in the nature of things, which reason and experience can discover. Both have a kind of a status in the nature of things, apart from our wishing it so. I assume that for one who begins with God, one must begin with an essential whole, with some concept of what is good for each individual in the context of the good for the whole of the creation, unified and held together in God.

The book *Habits of the Heart*,[1] which includes two hundred interviews of white middle-class citizens of the United States, reports that for the most part those interviewed reflect a belief in what the authors call onto-logical individualism. The only real reality for those interviewed is the iso-lated individual person. In their individuality, what these individuals seek is what is useful or what feels good. The authors call this stance utilitarian and expressive individualism. This would correspond in Tillich's analysis to individualization, dynamics, and freedom as self-initiation. One begins with one's self, with what one feels and wants, with what is useful to get what one wants. The ontological individualism revealed in *Habits of the Heart* represents or corresponds to McKeon's category of the phenomenal individual. McKeon would reserve the word *ontology* (or "science of be-ing," literally) to describe the individual with an essential nature or the whole with an essential nature, in which there are given structures to be discovered, uncovered, unearthed—something more than surface feelings or superficial reflection on experience.

Another useful analysis in reflecting on the meaning of and need for community is that of Talcott Parson's descriptions of the difference be-tween modern and traditional societies. Modern society is characterized by its emphasis on the universalistic aspects of our being, on those things that we have in common with other persons or animals. We break up life into its components parts, train persons to deal with some particular but uni-versally shared aspect of our existence, and then focus on that aspect in re-lating to persons. Thus a chiropodist treats our feet, an orthodontist straightens our teeth, and it seems we have enough different kinds of doc-tors to look after every part of the body. Each of us tries to learn more and more about less and less; we are valued for some special technical function that we can perform. And, as one who has had triple bypass surgery for my heart, I am aware of the value of this specialization. In a traditional soci-ety, the emphasis, Parsons claims, is on the individual as a particular indi-vidual with a particular history and a particular connection with things and persons. Others assess and respond to us as a whole. When I was growing up, the country doctor treated me as well as all the little parts of me. Now, I go to a different part of the hospital for everything that ails me.

A second characteristic of modernity is its focus on status by achievement, on what we have done or can do. In a traditional society, there is more focus on who we are, on what is called our ascribed status—the family into which we were born, our nationality, our ethnic group.

Third, in modern society, one attempts to maintain emotional distance from the persons with whom one works. Professional standards demand emotional distance or neutrality with all clients. Persons are clients. In a traditional society, one is involved with the whole person, with persons rather than clients. One lets oneself care for persons with whom one is related anyway.

Fourth, Parsons characterizes action in a traditional society by its diffuseness. The scope of interest in an object is broad, involving plurality of specific contexts, a plurality of instrumental or expressive interests in the object. In modern societies the scope of interest in an object is specific, capable of analytic separation from other interests in the object. I have become convinced that some combination or dialectical relationship between these principles is desirable.

The final, simplest, and for me most compelling perspective from which the nature of reality can be understood is that of the image of the body in Saint Paul's writings. In the twelfth chapter of First Corinthians, Paul makes it very clear that the Christian community is like a body in which all the parts are related to the other parts, in which each individual part is dependent on the other parts (see the previous section for additional discussion of this passage):

> Just as the body is one and has many members, and all the members of
> the body, though many, are one body, so it is with Christ. For by one
> Spirit we were all baptized into one body—Jews and Greeks, slaves or
> free—and all were made to drink of one Spirit. For the body does not
> consist of one member but of many. If the foot should say, "Because I
> am not a hand, I do not belong to the body," that would not make it
> any less a part of the body. And if the ear should say "Because I am
> not an eye, I do not belong to the body," that would not make it any
> less a part of the body. If the whole body were an eye, where would be
> the hearing? If the whole body were an ear, where would be the sense of
> smell? But as it is, God arranged the organs in the body, each one of
> them, as he chose. If all were a single organ, where would the body be?
> As it is, there are many parts, yet one body. The eye cannot say to the
> hand, "I have no need of you" nor again the head to the feet, "I have

*no need of you." On the contrary the parts of the body which seem to
be weaker seem to be indispensable, and those parts of the body which
we think less honorable we invest with the greater honor, and our
unpresentable parts are treated with greatest modesty, which our more
presentable parts do not require. But God has so adjusted the body,
giving the greater honor to the inferior parts, that there may be no
discord in the body, but that one member may have the same care for
one another. If one member suffers, all suffer together, if one member is
honored, all rejoice together (12:12–26).*

As discussed in the previous section, some claim that this image of
the body is only relevant for the church as the body of Christ, but not for
the world in general, not for the whole creation. I accept John's statements in the prologue to his gospel connecting Christ, the second person
of the Trinity, with the first person, God the Creator. We read,

*In the beginning was the Word [Christ], and the Word was God. He
was in the beginning with God; all things were made through him, and
without him was not made anything that was made. In him was life,
and the life was the light of men. The light shines in the darkness and
the darkness has not overcome it (1:1–5).*

From this conviction of John, I infer that Christ, the reality of
Christ, represents the intention of and the essence of the whole creation.
Hence, the image of the body in Paul can be taken to represent the intention of God for the universe, for everything. In Col. 1:15–20, Paul indicates the same understanding of creation:

*He [Christ] is the image of the invisible God, the first-born of all cre-
ation; for in him all things were created, in heaven and on earth, visible
and invisible, whether thrones or dominions or principalities or
authorities—all things were created through him and for him. He is before all things, and in him all things hold together. He is the head of the
body, the church: he is the beginning, the first-born from the dead, that
in everything he might be preeminent. For in him all the fullness of God
was pleased to dwell, and through him to reconcile to himself all things,
whether on earth or in heaven, making peace by the blood of his cross.*

For me, the fundamental image of the church is the fundamental image of
creation. The organic image of the body is the fundamental image of everything. It is the way in some sense things are, and the way things are
meant to be.

If we now look at the diagram of Paul Tillich's ontology, we see individualization, dynamics, and freedom on the left side and participation, form, and destiny on the right side. In his essay "The End of the Protestant Era," Tillich interprets the travail of the early and middle years of the twentieth century as the result of an overemphasis on individualization, dynamics, and freedom as self-initiation. The belief in democracy (citizen self-initiation), laissez-faire economics (in which the interactions of self-initiations are organized by market mechanisms), permissiveness in education (in which the student determines the content of a good education), and a Protestant emphasis not only on doing one's own believing but on believing whatever one wants to believe—all of these represent an overemphasis on one side of the ontological polarities. If Tillich is right about the structure of being, the results of this overemphasis have been disastrous: war, unemployment, conflict, personal disorganization, mental disorders, alcoholism, drugs, delinquency. All this personal and social disintegration is expected to continue to worsen. Communism and fascism can be seen as responses to the failure to balance the polarities and to take into account the need for participation, form, and destiny.

The authors of *Habits of the Heart* simply document this focus on individualization and self-initiation, an individualization without regard for any standards for self-initiation (form) or for any limits (destiny).

Tillich contends that we are at the end of the Protestant era, in which Luther's focus on freedom from the condemnation of the law was misinterpreted broadly as freedom from any law, from any limiting structures of reality. In his essay "Christian Liberty," Luther states that we are free from the condemnation of the law so that we can be free to choose to obey the law. At this point, we can call on the polar structure of being to introduce form and destiny and to connect the whole horizontal polar structure to the vertical dimension in which a connection with the underlying reality of the whole is called into play. Plato said it long ago: To be truly free is to choose freely to commit oneself to the good and the true and the beautiful. Luther said it also in his declaration that to be free is to be the slave of no one, except that the Christian, in freedom, chooses to be a slave of Christ—that is, to be a slave to the very structure of the creation that Christ participates in, points to, embodies, represents, intends, and is. To relax the tension between the need to be responsive to oneself and the need to choose to serve the Creator and the created structures of being is to guarantee disaster. To wallow in our own ideas, feelings, intuitions, perversions, and distortions of truth and goodness is not only to destroy ourselves but also the very conditions of life on the planet, as many are beginning to realize as they attend to the ecological crisis. The ecological cri-

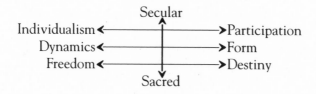

Paul Tillich
Ontological Polarities

Secular

Individualism ←————————→ Participation
Dynamics ←————————→ Form
Freedom ←————————→ Destiny

Sacred

Talcott Parsons

<u>Modern Society</u>	<u>Traditional Society</u>
Universalistic ←————————→	Particularistic
Status by achievement ←————————→	Status by ascription
Affective neutrality ←————————→	Emotional involvement (affectivity)
Specificity ←————————→	Diffuseness

Richard McKeon

<u>Phenomenal</u>	<u>Ontic</u>
Part (Hobbes)	Part (Erich Fromm)
Whole (Parsons)	Whole (Tillich)

sis is the single most obvious witness to our failure to take destiny into account. There is a structure to the physical, chemical, and biological life-support systems. Such structures are both given and not given because they are always in opposition to freedom, but freedom is equally limited by the structures that are in the nature of things. If we cannot live with this polarity, with this tension, we are likely to move just as disastrously in the opposite direction, thinking that there are once-for-all-time given structures, which, in being absolutized, become demonic.

Historical judgments are required to work out the balances of the polarities that are relevant for any particular period of history or for any particular situation. What is necessary to create or to restore a balance? Those who are now claiming that capitalism has proven itself right and just because of the collapse of the centralized economic systems and governments of Eastern Europe should not be surprised if history proves them wrong. If they attend to the social indices of disintegration and the ecological disasters now being predicted, they may understand that both

systems—one favoring freedom and one favoring centralized structure—
are more or less equally suspect. Unless we remain aware of the polar nature of reality, we are in for more and more trouble. Undoubtedly, the sin
underneath blind ideological advocacy and self-justification is deeper than
that beneath wrong ideology.

There is little hope as long as the dominant individuals in our world
are those who see reality in either/or terms, as either completely on the
left or completely on the right side of Tillich's polarities. Some current advocates of socialism, which has an emphasis historically on the right side,
are aware of the need to move toward the left. Advocates of capitalism,
with its emphasis historically on the left side, seem less willing now to admit the problems created by such an emphasis.

The ideological battle is useless, in my judgment, when fought without a recognition of the limitations of either side when overemphasized.
To believe that former socialist countries can now simply adopt a radical
left-sided emphasis can lead only to disaster. The industrial society of the
West, whether in its socialist or capitalist embodiments, has led to a demonic reality—the goal of unlimited economic growth.

Underlying all analyses that deal with these horizontal polarities in
relation to a certain time in history is Tillich's contention that the vertical
polarity of sacred and secular, or holy and profane, points to the underlying movement of life through all of history, from the first big bang to some
distant but relevant future. All space and all time provides the framework
for thinking about and responding to the present. The potentialities and
the consequences of being today must be brought into contact with that
which connects everything to everything, past, present, and future. That
reality we call God, or being itself, or the transcendent, or the ground of
being. This underlying reality is behind or beneath every action. The existence of a nation with 5 percent of the world's population using 25 percent
of the world's resources creates a problem if we begin with the thesis that
we are part of a whole such that whatever happens to anybody happens to
us. The ecological crisis further points to the underemphasis that industrial culture places on the structures of reality, the natural world, that cannot be ignored. In the destruction of these natural rhythms—such as the
destruction of the ozone as a protection from ultraviolet rays—we are experiencing the lack of attention to the whole within which we exist.

I contend that theology insists that we begin with the individual in
the context of the whole, a whole that has a life and meaning as a whole
and that can be ignored only at the price of individual frustration and destruction.

If we turn again to the figure on page 83 and examine Talcott Parson's perceptions of modern society, we can again see polarities that must be related (Parsons himself feels that modernity will dominate the future). I believe that a mixture of the principles of modern society and traditional society is needed today. Just how we can do that is not clear. There are no blueprints. There are no paths that simply have to be followed. But there is a direction. We must hack our paths out of the forests of the past and the present, of traditionalism and modernity.

In many ways, the fundamental decision facing humankind is the choice between an individualistic ontology and an ontology of the body, in which all parts are related to each other—including the part we call nature, the part we have treated as if it were merely a tool with no life of its own.

I conclude that we must either move toward accepting and strengthening our connection with all humankind and with nature or face increasing disintegration and destruction. On the positive side, such a move is the way to life, meaning, hope, being. We are called to establish the conditions for the development of the individual in community—in our churches and in the world. In 1977, a group began to set up those conditions within the context of University Church in Chicago. This led to the purchase of a twenty-one-flat building, the recruitment of members, the hammering out of a covenant, and a life together. We need more such efforts. My recent immersion in ecological issues has shown me the need to expand our understanding of the connection between the human community and the natural community as well as our material efforts to relate responsibly to the natural community.

Liberation Theology as a Resource

My first real contact with liberation theology was Paulo Freire's book, *Pedagogy of the Oppressed*. Freire emphasizes the importance of a process in which persons read the Bible in the light of their experience, finding in the Bible insights that help them understand the situation in which they exist. But I was never convinced that the so-called nondirective leadership provided by priests, catechists, and persons from outside the community did not provide a framework of interpretation to "help" the readers interpret the Bible—usually stemming in one way or another from Marxist categories and interpretations of the human situation.

Liberation theology arises out of the experience of oppression, of being determined in one's existence by forces outside oneself and by identifying groups of persons who feel this oppression more or less as a group. The main principles of liberation theology are as follows:

- Experiences of oppression are the starting point, not the Bible or traditions.
- The oppression is more than personal. It is understood to arise because of systems—social, economic, and political.
- The churches participate in this oppression as support systems for the oppressive forces, individually and collectively.
- A decision is made as to what is the fundamental reality around which the targets of oppression are located: they may be poor, women, or a particular ethnic group (race). The oppression is then labeled as classism, sexism, or racism. Locating the roots of the oppression requires some tools of analysis, some tools of social science.
- Only people who experience this oppression can be the basis for real discussion about what is happening and for change in the systems. (There has always been a dilemma in the Marxist movement because middle-class persons often led the organization of the proletariat. This continues to be a contradiction between theory and practice).
- The oppressors, the systems, cannot be changed by moral persuasion, by appeal to conscience. The systematic organization of the oppressed and the accumulation of power are necessary.
- Coalitions with other oppressed groups may follow after a particular group is organized in its own way, with its own program and leaders, and providing its own financial support. To accept money from other groups is to sell out to the enemy.

Black Liberation Theology—James Cone

James Cone, an African American, is Professor of Systematic Theology at Union Seminary in New York City.[2] It is interesting to note that there is not a single reference, so far as I can recall, to the environment in his 1984 book *For My People,* which I will use as a starting point to discuss black liberation theology; in my opinion, the next center for the organization of liberation theology will be the natural world.

For My People is about the meaning of the Christian faith from the standpoint of the African American struggle for liberation. This theology, known as black liberation theology, began in the second half of the 1960s out of the experience of African Americans who were economically exploited and politically marginalized. Says Cone:

> *If God is the creator of all persons, and through Christ has made salvation possible for everyone, why are some oppressed and segregated*

in the churches and in society on the basis of color? How can whites
claim Christian identity, which emphasizes love and justice of God, and
still support and tolerate the injustice committed against blacks by
churches and society? Why do blacks accept white interpretations of
Christianity that deny their humanity and ignore their own encounter of
God (extending back to Africa) as the liberator and protector of black
victims of oppression?[3]

Thus, neither the black nor the white churches are Christian.

The "issues to which theology addresses itself," Cone continues, "arise out of the life in society as persons seek to achieve meaning in a dehumanized world. . . . Theologians should not seek to do theology on the basis of scripture and traditions as if the existential and historical concerns of present-day humanity were non-existent."[4] The issues, says Cone, define theology. Issues arise out of social, historical, cultural, economic, and philosophical analysis.

African Americans thus looked at the issues of the time and began to think of the gospel of Jesus in terms of black power. The gospel of Jesus was seen as liberation from oppression. The cross represented God identifying with the victims of oppression. Resurrection was seen as the victory over oppression. God's Word was found "in the ghettoes and poverty-stricken villages of the world, in suffering with those who have no power,"[5] not in white seminaries or churches, not in middle-class black churches.

Black power became the dominant reality out of which black liberation theology developed. Black power was symbolized by the act of James Foreman, when on May 4, 1969, he walked down the aisle of Riverside Church in New York City with the Black Manifesto, which among other things demanded $500 million in reparations from the white churches and synagogues, "$15 per nigger."

As the movement away from dependence on and relation to whites developed, some black liberation theology advocates turned toward Africa as the root of black religious experience, as the source out of which black liberation theology might find new expression. This also represented a direction some black secular leaders took; Paul Robeson, for example, learned seven African languages to be able to experience the African spirit.

Moses became central. Salvation was rescue from Egypt. The Jesus of whites, a meek, pale-faced, blue-eyed Jesus, was rejected. Albert Cleague's *Black Jesus* represented the extent to which interpretations of the Christian faith went in rejecting the white Jesus. This book denied the whiteness of the Jew, Jesus, suggesting that Jesus had some African black blood.

Black liberation theology for Cone affirms God's unqualified solidarity with the poor in their fight against injustice. At first, black liberation theology had too little social analysis, rarely showing the links between racism, capitalism, and imperialism. There was too much moral outrage and appeal to the morality of the oppressors. This tactic was represented by the integrationist views of Martin Luther King, Jr., and Jesse Jackson. Cone came to see that system analysis was required. Furthermore, complete independence from the oppressor was necessary. The movement, he thought, should not be dependent on the oppressor for anything. "The absence of a comprehensive theological vision defined by the scientific tools of social analysis always leaves open the door to unchecked opportunism among those who claim to be leaders of the masses."[6]

Cone and his black liberation theology colleagues became disenchanted with everything white, especially of the white theologians under whom they had studied or whose theology they had more or less been forced to read in white seminaries. They wanted a theology that came out of their own history, out of black experience, out of spirituals, the blues, and sayings of their people. Barth, Tillich, and Pannenberg, some of the favorites among white theological students, were rejected as having nothing significant to say to their condition and the condition of their people.

There came a time when Cone began to realize the meaning of the Marxist thought that had been so influential among some Third World liberation theologians. He met with some of these theologians and read Third World liberation theologies. He began to see the connection between racism and international capitalism, colonialism, world poverty, classism, and sexism. Thus he grew to affirm that blacks cannot do adequate theology apart from their struggling brothers and sisters in the Third World.

Out of all of this, Cone developed what he describes as a new method of doing theology.

The first act of a theologian, says Cone, is both a religious and cultural affirmation and a political commitment on behalf of the liberation of the poor and voiceless. The first question about any theologian is the quality of this commitment. Praxis, a reflective political action, comes before theology. The theologian starts with the identification with the misery of the black, the African, the Hispanic American, the Asian, the Latin American, the Minjungb (South Korean).

Theology does not begin with a reflection on divine revelation as if the God of our faith is separate from the suffering of our people. Truth is found in the histories, cultures, and religions of our people:

How can we speak about Jesus' death on the cross without first speaking about the death of the poor? How can the poor of our countries achieve worth as human beings in a world that has attempted to destroy our cultures and religions?. . . In their worship the God of grace and judgment meets the poor, transforms their personhood from nobody to somebody, and bestows on them power and courage to struggle for justice.[7]

Worship is a community happening, "not primarily an expression of an individual's private relationship to God." It is "an eschatological invasion of God into the gathered community of victims, empowering them with the 'divine spirit from on high,' 'to keep on keeping on,' even though the odds might appear to be against them."[8]

For Cone, both black and Third World liberation theology can be understood as beginning with the commitment to liberate the poor from their oppression, by performing a social analysis that locates the root of the oppression. In light of this social analysis, the Bible becomes a living word speaking to the situation of the oppressed, a truth that must be expressed in new forms, with concepts and words and songs out of the oppressed peoples' pasts. Black liberation theology must take this world theology seriously because, for Cone, there will be no liberation of African Americans without the liberation of Third World peoples. This reflects the point of view developed by Malcolm X, namely, that there would be no liberation of American blacks without the help of black persons in Africa. Liberation of all oppressed persons seems to be the direction in which Cone is moving. Another strong point of the Third World liberation theologians' perspective is their use of Marxist thought as a tool for analysis of the dominant economic forces that are strangling the Third World and that control the First World. Cone believes that theologians must take seriously this tool for social analysis.

Finally, Cone asks the question, where do black theologians and black church leaders go from here? He suggests that the black churches need a new vision produced by the black church without assistance from white theologians or white resources of any kind. A team should be crated to act independently of white liberals and middle-class black interests. Such a team would embody the following principles:

- Black unity is to be achieved by the affirmation of black history and culture. Loving what is black does not mean hating whites.
- Include the best of the integrationist movement as articulated by Martin Luther King, Jr. The beloved community is the goal.
- Half of the team should be women to embody an antisexist stance.

- The team should focus on democracy and socialism, including the Marxist critique of monopoly capitalism. The necessities of life are inalienable rights.
- There must be a global vision that includes the Third World.

The best in the black religion should be affirmed, embracing the creative elements in the religions of the poor all over the globe. Martin Luther King, Jr., and Malcolm X embody the best examples of the black religions that attempt to combine religious vision with political commitment to social transformation.

Nature Liberation Theology

What is particularly interesting about Cone's position to one who is focused on the present crying of the earth is the emphasis on beginning with some analysis of what is taking place, on placing ourselves where we can hear the groaning of the oppressed reality. Thus, I insist that we as Christians or as citizens listen to what is being communicated to us by the results of our actions in destroying the physical, chemical, and biological basis for life. Faithwise, we can say that God is using the natural world to tell us something, to open our eyes to the destructiveness of our way of life, to bring judgment, if you will, upon what we seek to be, do, possess, and enjoy.

So, just as Cone says we must listen to our social scientists, I say we must listen to our earth scientists to understand what is happening or is likely to happen to our air, water, soil, trees, crops, ozone, and climate. I also think that we must listen to our social scientists to try to understand why we are not able to respond to the crisis of the natural order.

We need a coalition that includes those who are suffering oppression and death because of our social organizations and the values represented through them and the persons who have chosen to identify themselves with the crying of the earth. Granted, the latter group for the most part does not experience the same catastrophic results as the poverty-stricken persons of all nations or those who are oppressed because of race or gender. The exceptions to this, of course, are those who live under the threat of toxic wastes both from productive enterprises and from nuclear plants. There is no question that their situation is existential in the same sense that class and race and gender crate existential situations of oppression. As more and more persons suffer the results of ozone depletion (some scientists expect two out of three Australians to have skin cancer by the age of seventy), they too will begin to feel as if they are oppressed, without any real control over the destruction of the ozone that is threatening their lives.

I predict that before long there will be an increasing number of persons who live under threats caused by the productive enterprises of the Western industrial society. Flooding will occur, shorelines will disappear, storms will increase in intensity, climate will be even more unpredictable, crops will fail, food shortages will increase, and the number of those affected by cancer will grow as carcinogens from pesticides and wastes permeate the water system and are ingested directly. Oppression will be a nearly universal phenomena. Environmental issues know no boundaries of class, or race, or gender. All persons are in somewhat the same situation with regard to ozone depletion and global warming (although most toxic waste dumps are near the homes of minorities or poor whites).

Having experienced connections with some of the world at the 1992 Earth Summit conference in Rio de Janeiro, I understand better than ever that our hope for change comes from the world community—from the German people who have seen the Black Forest disintegrate, the indigenous peoples of Brazil who have witnessed the destruction of their homelands, the Indian people displaced and poisoned by huge dams and the accompanying industries, the Eastern European people who live with health problems created by their industries. There is an opportunity to mobilize internationally.

I affirm that the general principles of liberation theology with which this discussion began are even more relevant than has as yet been recognized by most of us. No one, of course, can any longer believe that a change in the ownership of the means of production will automatically deal with the issue of justice. This is not to say that governmental intervention in economic life is not required. In fact, it is clearer than ever that intervention is necessary by governments and citizens. The issue is whether or not the intervention is effective, efficient, democratic, humane, and rooted in an understanding of being in which we are in communion with each other, nature, and God.

A Christian Theological Perspective on the Ecological Crisis: Douglas John Hall

In *Imaging God: Dominion as Stewardship*, Douglas John Hall insists that the environmental issues of our time will not become a priority for the churches unless there is a new understanding of being underlying efforts to respond.

Hall's search for such an ontology focuses on what he designates as the biblical ontology, the tradition of Jerusalem, as compared to the tradition of Athens. The real issue is "who we understand ourselves to be." We need to change our understanding as the basis for changing our way of being and for explaining and supporting these changes. The concept around which his considerations are organized is "the image of God."

For Hall, all knowing has a historical dimension. All biblical interpretation is a search for meanings in the context of the historical situation. All search for moral imperatives is a search in the context of dynamic, changing historical situations. The Word of God is always addressed to a particular person or community in a particular situation. I think that Hall would agree with my interpretation of God as not being bound by the Bible, at the same time that the Bible is a prism through which the Word for our time shines, is heard, is received. I am sure that Hall would also see the reception of the Word as involving a communal dimension. The community of the faithful listens together even as it pays special attention to individual hearings of the Word.

For Hall, to be in the image of God is to be in relation to God, other persons, and the natural world. Each one of these types of relationships is distinct and yet related. To be in relation to one of these realms or dimensions is to be in relation to all of them. The character of the relationship is designated by the concept of love—love not simply as an emotion, but love as a movement with, for, and in communion with other realities.

This image is not something that one possesses, something that happens once and for all time. It is a process. It involves a daily movement. It is not an endowment. One is in the image of God when one relates. To understand this concept, I have always thought of Martin Luther, whose life seemed to be a falling in and out of relation with God. We are created to be with (coexistence), for (proexistence), and together with (communion, community, covenant) other realities. In our distorted, fallen humanity, we are alone, being against (estrangement, alienation), above (pride, attempt at mastery, domination), or below (sloth, escape from responsibility) other realities.

Reason, will, moral decisions—all are tools that can be used to relate, but the possession of them does not mean that one is in the image of God. Therefore, the distinction between humans and other creatures is broken down.

The character of our relationship with other realities is given by the character of being of Jesus. Hierarchy and domination are rejected, Hall claims, by Jesus: "The rulers of the gentiles lord it over them and their great men exercise authority over them. It shall not be so among you; but whoever will be great among you will be your servant" (Matt. 20:25–26). Hall's point is that the concept of dominion in Gen. 1:26, however one interprets the meaning of the Hebrew word translated by *dominion,* must be superseded by the understanding of the character of relationships embodied and advocated by Jesus. The Old Testament's understandings should be placed in the context of the tradition of Jerusalem, in the context of the life and teachings of Jesus.

Our exploitation and rape of the earth—our broken relationship with the natural world—results both from our notion of who we are and from our failure to be what we know we are created and called to be.

Underlying our understanding of ourselves as the image of God is an understanding of the nature of God. Hall claims that much of the Christian tradition understands God to be completely transcendent, all-powerful, all-controlling, all-knowing, all-fulfilled God, whose only desire is for praise. Such a God stands above the ebb and flow of the creation. But such a God, Hall contends, is not the only God depicted in the stories and historical events found in the Bible. There is another God, who participates in all of the creation with joy and suffering, pain and rejoicing. For Hall, God is a loving, caring, compassionate presence, waiting for the opportunity to be with, for, and in communion with the creation, especially, but not exclusively, with us.

I would push Hall a little further than I think he goes, describing God as participating in our lives and in the creation as a whole, with the suffering, rejoicing, and becoming of all reality in some sense also being God's becoming. Hall certainly focuses on the participation. To be for, with, and in communion with each other and with nature is to be for, with, and in communion with God, and vice versa. Hall quotes the twentieth chapter of First John, holding that one does not love God unless one loves his or her neighbor and the natural world.

For some, God is a completely fulfilled reality without potentiality waiting to be fulfilled. God has actualized all possibilities, "needing" nothing. For others, God grows, increases in being, becomes more. Thus we do not become whole, fulfilled, sanctified alone. As we are fulfilled, we become in the image of God, and God is also fulfilled.

The implications of the relational view of the image of God are widespread, both theologically and sociologically. Ontologically, we are individuals in community. Soteriologically, the notion that we are "saved" or fulfilled individually is called into question. If we take Paul seriously, as Hall does in appealing to the image of the body in 1 Cor. 12:14–26, the shared nature of our pilgrimage is clear even though the notion that we are responsible and judged as individuals (according to Matt. 25:31–46) is maintained. The dialectic of the individual in community (human and nonhuman) makes it difficult to evade responsibility for all of existence. It is also difficult to be above or below our neighbors because ontologically we are one with and alongside of our neighbors. The notion that we are parts of each other, absorbing each other's being at the same time that we are separate, has always been helpful to me. The interrelatedness of the dimensions of existence—human, nonhuman, divine—elevates the nonhuman, giving it a sacredness or an enchantment by spirit that changes our judgment of its importance both for us and for itself and for God. Ultimately, environmental issues, then, especially as they involve the material foundation of human existence, will be responded to creatively only if we respond from the perspective of an enchanted earth, an earth to which we and God are related in a holy triangle in which the way we relate to one part of the triangle reflects the way we respond to the others. We cannot love God without loving each other and the earth, we cannot love the earth without loving God and each other, and we cannot love each other without loving the earth and God.

4

Being a Part of a Creation Community

The Calling in Our Congregations

If what I have said thus far is in the direction of the truth, we are living in a new age that might be characterized as the age of creation focus or the age of the thrice-born Christian. The second birth is the age of justification by faith, faith in our being accepted in spite of our unacceptability. No matter what we think and feel and have done or not done, we are accepted because of who we are, children of God, created in the image of God. What is required of us is simply trust and acceptance of our dependence. The third birth is a birth into the acceptance of our connectedness with the rest of the world, human and nonhuman, at a deep level, even though at the empirical level we act and feel isolated and unconnected. We are called to act and think and feel as if we belong to each other and to the universe. The church has the opportunity to respond to the environmental revolution as if to be in the image of God is to be and act as if we were in relation to everybody and everything.

Nurturing this connectedness with each other has been a major function of many Christian churches. What is somewhat new for some and completely new for others is the attention to how we are for, with, and in communion with the nonhuman part of the creation. While the dimensions, human and nonhuman, are quite inseparable for me, here I will focus on the way in which connections with the nonhuman parts of creation might be the focus for organizing the life of our churches, individually and collectively.

95

The first function of the churches in response to the environmental revolution is to provide access to what God is saying to us through what is happening to the natural world. This means an educational program that attends to what is happening to the nonhuman parts of the creation, the physical, chemical, biological cradle of life.

A second role of the churches is to provide a self-understanding of the Christian faith in which the concept of the image of God as relational is explored. Theological education is crucial.

A third function of the churches in regard to environmental issues is to explore, with lay persons taking a leading role, the meaning of the calling in our personal lives, our living situations, our work situations, our economic and political systems. They should also help us examine our calling in general, our calling to be in covenant in a creation community.

There are several levels of activity. Congregations can embody a creation focus. Either in denominations or in ecumenical organizations, retreat centers for lay training in the workplace can be initiated.

Congregations or denominations can form life communities to move intentionally toward a lifestyle that is a foretaste of the future. Most congregations are not in a favorable position to move as far and as fast as what is called for here.

At the ecumenical level, the churches can provide some leadership for a people's movement to confront the economic giants with protest and encouragement for new directions, first in broad environmental responsibility and then in the direction of human responsibility. It may well be that new societal systems will emerge from all of this, systems in which the organizing reality is a serious covenantal relationship.

I know a few churches that are seriously involved in becoming creation awareness centers, earth community congregations, or care for the creation churches. Special ministries are being established in national and regional areas. Denominational agencies are preparing statements and directives. There is much going on of which I am not yet aware. Undoubtedly, it would be useful to have a survey of the actual state of affairs. My impression is that churches are beginning to get involved but that we have miles to go. My suggestions in this section are based on some forty years of experience in social ministries in churches at several levels and on a few concrete movements established by church bodies.

In my experience, the key to movement is to encourage a few people to focus for a period of years on a particular project of ministry, in this case on the environment. Because the environmental movement is so large, further focus is desirable. Focus is very difficult for the churches, especially when they feel responsible for everybody and everything. The second important aspect of ministry is to focus on education (a special Bible study and educational meeting once a week, for example) in the context of action, what I call connections. In my own church, a focus on Central America involved many person's trips to the area, sanctuary for two Guatemalan families over several years, sister parishes in Central America, connections with other churches locally and nationally that were involved in the same kind of mission, participation in demonstrations, communication with legislators, connection with secular groups with the same focus, a separate budget, a four-year mission as assistant to the Lutheran Bishop of El Salvador, special staff, and innumerable special services and events.

As I have sought to communicate about the environment with hundreds of persons at Holden Village and with my own church members, I have found that there is no one way to address persons. Some are ready to act immediately. Others want to understand the theological issues. Some are more involved in relating to the natural world on an experiential basis. Some are a long way from home and will not move into a new way of thinking about their lives. I do not know a community that represents a way of being relevant for the future and also addresses the social and institutional changes required to shift destructive practices that threaten a sustainable future. The most comprehensive statement of intent that I have found is that of Riverside Church (see the appendices).

Where the focus on the creation has not started, the first challenge is to find or to become engaged in a study of the issues, using the 1992 or 1993 edition of the Worldwatch Institute's *State of the World* or Al Gore's *Earth in the Balance.* An alternative is *Scientific American*'s September 1989 edition, published as *Managing Planet Earth.* Further suggestions for materials appear in the bibliography.

Alternatively, the pastor could be the first one to begin to listen more attentively to what planet earth is saying. It might be helpful to put one of the suggested texts in the hands of your pastor as soon as you can. Give your pastor some materials, but not too much. What is important, I believe, is to encourage your pastor to listen to the voices of the environmental revolution as if they were the Word of God to the congregation. Theological and philosophical texts, experiences in the wilderness, action books, personal stories—all are important, but no substitute for the "new data," the discovery of the Word of God in and through the creation.

At the same time, have available one or more of the how-to texts suggested in the bibliography. Persons do not want to be left with the sense of an immense problem without learning something that can be done about it. You might want to make copies of the suggestions for living toward the future or some of the other materials in the appendices of this book. It is also important to convey the notion that God appreciates, savors, smiles when small steps are taken. The book *Fifty Simple Things To Do To Save the Earth* is a nonthreatening introduction to action.

Some people will already be taking action. It is important that who-ever is taking the lead is already doing or begins to do some of the things sketched in the appendices. Many people are already recycling and will re-act negatively if you assume that nothing is being done, especially if you are, as I am, a Johnny-come-lately to the environmental movement. Some will find fault with what you are doing, especially if you are talking about changes that threaten established tastes and habits, such as driving cars, flying in airplanes, eating meat, and buying clothes. It is impossible to es-cape inconsistencies. I find that my friends want to give me T-shirts with environmental messages, the wearing of which for me is a contradiction to my sense that we should resist the consumerism represented by the promo-tion of such buying. They also frequently accuse me of using a lot of trees in the course of my photocopying to communicate about environmental issues.

If it seems appropriate, at some point the pastor can be encouraged to preach occasional sermons on God and the creation, preferably after she or he has taken some basic steps toward environmental responsibility.

A theological basis for whatever is done is essential. For me, the most helpful theological discussion is Douglas John Hall's *Imaging God: Domin-ion as Stewardship*. This book is out of print, and it may take some effort to find it in libraries. But it is worth the effort. This book combines sophisti-cated biblical and historical theological analysis with an awareness of spe-cific environmental issues. Hall's *The Steward: Biblical Symbol Come of Age* is also useful. Increasingly, I feel that a study course on a book dealing with the theology of creation, such as Hall's text, is essential to provide churches with the depth of understanding required for sustained attention to the environment. The more personal we can be with indicating what God is saying to us, the better. Some texts are listed in the bibliography.

All of this may or may not precede a meeting of interested persons that is announced in the church bulletin well in advance. Hopefully, it will receive a word of support from the pastor. It helps to have the pastor and at least one of the respected members of the congregation involved in the call for a meeting. Ecological matters are now recognized as a matter for everyone's attention. Such matters are no longer on the fringe of public discussions. Many churches and church members, however, are a long way from appreciating what is going on in God's world. If one is too enthusiastic, one soon gets labeled and sometimes ignored as an ecofreak.

It is important to have some of the resources already in hand or even distributed to some persons before such a meeting. The materials available are vast. Usually, I find that some people know a good deal more than I do about the issues involved. They should be asked to lead sessions.

In our church, progress seems to be made most rapidly if the result is a series of meetings at some time most church members can come if they choose. A lot depends on where persons are in their encounter with materials. The old-timers fret at going over materials that I think are essential for newcomers to the issues. At some point, some action should be considered. Some persons always prefer to act rather than to read or to discuss. As soon as a number of persons indicate that they are aware of the actions that can be taken or have read one of the how-to books, one should have a brainstorming session dealing with the life of the church—to inventory the ecological/energy-efficient things that are already being done and to make a list of additional things that could be done. At this session, it is important to involve persons who are connected with different aspects of the church's life, if you can get them: pastor, secretary, sexton, church school teachers, leaders in various auxiliaries. I have put a copy of our inventory in the appendices.

The aim of this discussion should be to begin to formulate what is being done and what might be done. First, it is vital to recognize everything that is being done. Communicate the results via bulletins and newsletters in a way that is not overwhelming. Every new action should be formulated as a suggested action for further consideration.

It is desirable, but difficult, to have different members of your task force focus on different issues and begin to read more widely.

At some point, one could enlist persons of the church who are parts of other activities to act on behalf of the environment, or one could assign members of the task force to make contacts with other organizations working on the issues. It might be useful to invite leaders of other community activities to present their programs.

I have always found it useful, if the group catches on, to have a few members meet regularly to discuss what is happening and what might happen. To do this in the larger group may or may not be wise. The problem is to find a time. At one point, we had a 7:30 A.M. breakfast planning meeting for two or three groups, such as the Care for the Creation Task Force, that were running simultaneously. We met almost continuously for four years. We also made this more than just planning; we spent some time talking about what had happened in our own lives that week.

At some point, one will want to move toward a statement or covenant that indicates the direction in which the church is committed to move. There are examples of such statements in the appendices from Riverside Church in New York City and from Holden Village in Chelan, Washington. Part of the value of such statements is in the process of producing them. A group might rework one of these examples.

There may be an opportunity at your church to present a speaker on the issues at some time when a fair portion of the congregation is likely to be present.

Whatever you do, do not expect everyone or even a majority of church members to get involved. If three or four members get enthused and committed, something significant may happen over a period of time. Also accept little steps toward responsible action with enthusiasm. If someone starts using cloth handkerchiefs instead of facial tissue, you should rejoice—just as you should if someone takes recycling seriously or stops eating meat.

While you are attending to the earth, stop periodically to read some of the materials on the theology of creation that root what you are doing in the Bible. See the bibliography for some suggestions.

Begin to contact organizations working on the issues; encourage different members to subscribe to different publications.

Establish a budget for the activity. In the beginning, you may have to provide resources. Put projects in your personal budget. Encourage members to do the same. Encourage some new persons to come to meetings. Use the task force as a way to attract persons to the church. Consider carefully how your work is a threat to the life of the church, even as you do not let that anxiety be the determining factor in decisions. This kind of work must eventually involve a good portion of the church, or it will not meet the challenge of the ecological crisis. You need to find a way to put materials in the hands of interested persons, and you should not expect them to pay for everything.

Look for meetings and conferences to which members of your task force may go. Our church had three persons at the Earth Summit in Rio de Janeiro, contributing two thousand dollars to one. There are all kinds of things happening in many communities. Send someone to some conferences; agree in the group to help finance trips, even if it stretches your budget. For our Central American project, one family in our church gave a trip to Central America as a college graduation present, and the father went along. This young man became involved and has been back several times. Enlist young persons.

Begin to collect materials and find ways to use them in the worship services: prayers, hymns, liturgies. Use them in church school classes also. Contribute to lenten books and such materials that reach a wider audience. Participate in planning the church school curriculum.

Secure videotapes, audiotapes, and other resources that can be used with groups in your church or elsewhere. Encourage the use of such resources in homes.

Eventually, have a group visit your congressional representatives to explore their thinking on some of the subjects. Further still, churches might turn part of their grounds into community organic gardens.

It is crucial that such activity be understood in the context of forming a cell of the church in which the interest in the natural world is related to interest in the full range of spirit, one's own deep self, others, nature, and God. To be "in the spirit" is to be with, for, and in communion with the whole creation. Such faith should show in the manner of the environmentalist. Meditation and prayer are an essential part of the environmental revolution.

Part of the calling of the churches is to nurture an awareness of the ecological crisis in their members. There are scores of books and articles that suggest hundreds of things to do and be in order to care for creation. I have many of these actions in the appendices. In order not to be overwhelmed by these lists, I suggest that you set aside a time each day to think about a couple of the items. An alternative is to look at the items until you find one that you want to do something about. I can summarize the meaning of all these listed items in the following ten commandments for caring for the earth:

- Thou shalt begin every day by thinking about and praying for and with the universe. Find a symbol for the universe or the earth—a picture, a globe. Think concretely of some place or of some events with which you are increasingly familiar. Where are the forty thousand kids under age five dying from starvation and related diseases every day? What is happening to the air quality of your community?

- Thou shalt save energy. Cut your energy use by at least 20 percent for the first year. Turn off lights, replace incandescent bulbs with fluorescent ones, walk, bicycle, carpool, reduce the number of car trips, drive a high-mileage car.

- Thou shalt recycle.

- Thou shalt listen to what the scientists are telling us about the air, earth, and water. Read each day from *State of the World;* from *In Context, World Watch,* or *Amicus* magazines; or from Al Gore's *Earth in the Balance.*
- Thou shalt choose to use less: less gasoline, less fuel for heat and hot water, less meat, less food, fewer plastics, fewer new paper products, fewer books and magazines, fewer new clothes.
- Thou shalt be part of a group committed to caring for the creation—a task force in your congregation, a group of students at school, or a group living on your block or in your apartment building or community.
- Thou shalt covenant a part of your budget to projects that help persons care for the creation.
- Thou shalt communicate with your friends and enemies, distribute literature, subscribe to a magazine for someone else (or better, loan your own copy of the magazine)—always being, of course, judicious in your use of resources.
- Thou shalt expose yourself to the world of nature, to forests and mountains, to garbage dumps, to agricultural processes, to feedlots, to organic farming.
- Thou shalt be open to accepting the ecological crisis as a gift, as an opportunity for new experiences and new ways of being with, for, and in communion with other persons and with the whole of creation.

One of the ways to bring the church environmental movement together with the issue of poverty is to begin to connect with persons in poorer countries. Churches can sponsor relationships with individuals in another country, a country that may be a focus for several church members or for the church. Relationships with persons from this country who are in the United States may lead to relationships with the disadvantaged here. All sorts of relationships are possible. In the fifties, I knew a suburban church that was related to five churches in a nearby urban area. Presbyters were exchanged. The suburban church members taught church school and participated in many ways in the city churches. On occasion, the members all met together. One mark of faithful witness might be whether or not a congregation has sister churches in developing countries and in the disadvantaged sections of our country. If so, there is more chance that the body of Christ will be Christ's body. Missionaries could help provide for these connections.

Keep in mind that one cannot live without participating in some degree in the destruction of the creation—and that it is almost impossible to avoid some contradictions in your lifestyle. I recently flew to Rio de Janeiro for the Earth Summit for example, burning lots of jet fuel. At the same time, I insisted that my wife and son not drive but take the train to Seattle to use much less gasoline (thus reducing carbon emissions). In another example, I arranged to make a special trip to the store to buy some Tofu Scrambler. When I was writing the above commandments, however, I realized how insensitive I had been to make a special trip for one item. The need for grace abides, especially in the area of ecological crisis; we need what I call penultimate grace, the grace that helps us live with our contradictions and ambiguities, even with the best of intentions.

All of the suggestions discussed in this section are relevant for how we as individuals respond to the ecological crisis through churches, schools, and clubs as well as in our homes. We will now consider separately how we can respond in work situations because of the crucial role of such responses in the environmental movement.

The Calling in Our Work Lives

After the Second World War, the German Evangelical churches (the state churches of Germany) organized what were known as Evangelical Academies in each of the German states. I visited several of these in 1955. The purpose of the academies was to create a new thrust in German life, spearheaded by the Christian faith and focused on the way individuals could carry this faith out into their workplaces. People were recruited for retreats, conferences, and consultations on the basis of their roles or functions in the workplace. Thus, doctors, lawyers, elementary school teachers, secretaries of executives, executives in electricity-producing companies, executives of steel mills, labor leaders, and many more groups came to discuss how they might be responsible for a new Germany. Just so, we could establish such centers in which the focus might be, at least in the beginning, on what could be done about the ecological crisis. There are many other critical issues, of course, poverty being (in my estimation) the next most crucial one.

I can imagine such a conference with, for example, the executives of the Commonwealth Edison Electric Company of Chicago; some officers of other electric utility companies; Cardinal Bernadine of Chicago; Amory Lovins of the Rocky Mountain Institute; the head of the Pacific Power and Light Company, who has provided creative leadership in the direction of energy efficiency; and, undoubtedly, a number of others who have taken leadership, along with many who have not.

Some companies are already taking action. The head of the power company is Osage, Iowa, has taken the lead in cleaning up their production processes while saving residents of Osage more than one thousand dollars per family. The 3M company of Minnesota is well-known for having reduced its production of chemical wastes and in the process saved itself hundreds of thousands of dollars because the executives decided to explore the possibilities.

It is clear to me that Christian churches avoid their responsibility if they do not proclaim the requirements of faith in very specific terms. Of course, they get into trouble when they try to be concrete and specific about the content of the moral imperative, especially if they insist on labeling a particular view of such an imperative as Christian. But that is what they are called to do in love. The content of the Christian imperative seems to be more unclear today than it ever has been. Risks are involved in working out the content of our calling. Therefore, we need to develop a mechanism in which the lay members who know about the concrete situations must work together with the theologians and Christian leaders who know about the broad demands of the faith to hammer out what Christian responsibility for the environment means.

The value of this process is inestimable because, if planned well, the clergy become aware both of the possibilities and the problems of their parishioners. Then they can with more clarity understand the need to proclaim both grace and law, the latter reluctantly but definitely proclaimed. Then, and then only, do they become aware of the real opportunities and limitations. They also then understand the ambiguities and the essential role of the proclamation of God's overflowing grace.

During my affirmative action work with Jesse Jackson and Operation Breadbasket (which later became Operation PUSH), we learned that corporations that wanted to be responsible formed task forces on affirmative action and appointed able personnel with authority and budgets. These persons had their status and salaries dependent on producing results. They also needed to be directly responsible to the CEO if they were to achieve results. In addition, reviews of their work periodically needed to be reported in the presence of the CEO.

Thus, a major thrust of the work of a denominational or interdenominational church organization focusing on the workplace should be toward enlisting the help of the heads of corporations. Things can be done and leadership can be exercised at all levels, however. Job Ebenezer of the United Lutheran Church of America was able to achieve significant results at the level of the physical operation of the headquarters office. He now has been given official recognition, having responsibility for helping the whole denominational life attend to the issues of the environment.

One of the first questions to ask about one's work is that of the significance of what is produced where one works. In some of my discussions about this, persons have said that they would not work for the weapons industry, for a cigarette factory, for a casino, for an advertising agency, in coal mining, in clothes sales (especially where fashion was emphasized), in the manufacture and sale of luxury items, and for media other than public radio or television. Much of our work will thus be rejected as a faithful response to God's call.

An equally important question is, what types of work could be considered Christian vocations?

One's response to these questions depends on whether or not one has a view of the environmental revolution in which the destructive consequences of the lifestyle of the industrialized nations is questioned in general, and that of the United States is questioned in particular. Whatever promotes excessive consumption must be challenged in view of the long-term effects of the use of nonrenewable sources and the excessive emissions of polluting substances.

There are opportunities in most work situations for persons to take some initiative. Recycling, using recycled products, using reusable equipment, copying on both sides, cutting down on full-sheet memos—all kinds of little things can be done. I have never seen the environmental inventory of a manufacturing plant similar to the one for churches in Appendix E. Undoubtedly, it would be useful for someone to gather these inventories and make them available to those of us who are interested in working seriously with our parishioners. We could thus move beyond the little things while we celebrate everything that we can do, however small the effect on the environmental crisis.

The Calling in Economics and Politics

Thus far, I have discussed mostly actions at the level of personal responsibility: what can we do as individuals in our various existing relationships? In all cases, I have assumed that the churches will be functioning as catalysts and as support groups for the individuals moving in the directions suggested. Of course, some individuals will use other organizations as the support group, and some will move more or less on their own. Now, I will address the economic institutions.

At the Earth Summit meetings in Rio de Janeiro, the twenty-eight hundred representatives of nongovernmental organizations were divided into thirty-one task forces. My group considered alternative economic models. Our conversations focused on alternatives to the present economic systems, but some of us insisted that there was no way suddenly to transform these systems. Therefore, we had to consider intervening in the present systems with intermediary, transitional goals, which, of course, could turn out to be fairly permanent.

The principles developed by our group were these:

1. The fundamental purpose of economic organization is to provide for the basic needs of a community, in terms of food, shelter, education, health, and the enjoyment of culture as opposed to a concentration on the generation of profit and the growth of production for its own sake. Economic life must also be organized in such a way that it enhances rather than destroys the environment and safeguards resources for the use of future generations.

2. An alternative to the current system must be based on indigenous, community-based, people-empowering models that are rooted in person's experiences, histories, and ecocultural realities. This implies incorporating alternative productive systems, decision-making processes, and technologies, especially those drawn from indigenous peoples and peasant communities.

3. An alternative economic model must recognize and institutionalize a central and equal role for women in shaping economic life.

4. An alternative economic model must be based on the relative self-sufficiency of communities, regions, and nations, rather than on free trade, the world market, and large domestic and transnational corporations as the central institutions that determine production and distribution.

5. Economic life must be informed by bottom-up development strategies, in which persons and communities have the power to make economic decisions that affect their lives, in contrast with the dominant model, which marginalizes communities and fosters international economic relations in which the center subjugates the periphery.

6. One of the central ethical foundations of an alternative model is the interdependence of all peoples, communities, and the nonhuman material world. This interdependence demands a system of sharing resources based on autonomy, equality, participatory democracy, and solidarity. As members of a community, individuals must also take responsibility for living within the limits of the earth's resources, in contrast with the developed countries' model of excessive consumption.

7. Human and economic development indicators should no longer exclusively or principally reflect material growth and technological advance but must take into account individual, social, and environmental well-being. Such indicators would include general health, gender equalities, unpaid family leave, equal distribution of income, better care of children, and the maximization of human happiness with minimal use of resources and minimal generation of waste.

8. In an alternative economic system, the state will be transformed from being chiefly a facilitating agent of the present economic system, which is dominated by domestic and transnational corporations, into a mechanism that genuinely represents and serves the people's interests and promotes a strategy of self-reliant, community-centered development.

The political commitment of the participants was as follows:

1. Returning to and identifying ourselves with our grassroots communities to realize collective self-reliance and establish alternative, community-based economic models.

2. Building mutually empowering mechanisms and institutions to establish an alternative economic order.

3. Participating in building a people's environmental movement, starting from bioregional networks and alliances and moving toward global solidarity.

As you can see from these goals, there was no discussion of the way in which attending to the people's interests will automatically take into account the environmental issues. The importance of these goals for me is in the awareness that there is an urgent need for rethinking traditional economics. The present economic and political systems simply do not work to protect the environment.

Responsible members of creation communities can thus move in two directions. First, they can locate and identify with those communities that are already at work in building an alternative system of economic life. Present communities should be supported, helped, expanded in their vision, and even joined. For example, my own community of about sixty people, formed in 1979, could grow from being primarily concerned with each other to being concerned with the earth. It could also develop more economic thrust than it now has.

Second, the creation communities, the churches, and other communities that share in the concern for the creation could be encouraged to intervene in the present economic system. The Earth Summit and the preparatory meeting provided some opportunity to work in this direction on several levels. For instance, our working groups proposed the organization of a people's Green movement. There is need for a vehicle that puts pressure on economic and political institutions.

The churches again can be the catalysts for this and at a crucial point will need to take a leading role, but the organization will need to be separate from the churches.

The first task is to organize the greens, that is, those persons who have begun to understand the seriousness of the ecological crisis. These persons should be organized in a worldwide network to negotiate with the economic institutions chiefly, but no means solely, responsible for the ecological crisis.

For seven years, I worked with Jesse Jackson and his program to bring affirmative action to corporate America. Teams of preachers, with the help of some staff, approached corporations with a view to negotiating covenants in which African Americans would find more economic opportunities than before. Corporations responded in various ways. Occasionally, we organized the African American community and their friends to withhold their buying power from a corporation to encourage it to take us seriously and to respond with some serious reorganization. The covenants included job opportunities, promotions, legal services, insurance services, advertising services, banking services, philanthropy, high-level positions, the development of new and existing suppliers, counseling services, computer services, cleaning services, and everything else that is involved in a business. There is no reason, I believe, why we could not negotiate with corporate America—in fact, with corporations worldwide—for an environmental program that is friendly to the earth. With the growth of transnational corporations, the negotiating teams could represent the peoples of more than one country and thus help build a people's worldwide network.

The essential role of the churches and religious groups is in providing the moral leadership that cannot easily be associated with special interests. Preachers and religious leaders, with the help of sophisticated staffs, could learn what goals are realistic and could become agents for social change without the stigma of being a governmental program, so violently resisted, especially in the United States.

The environmentalists have three kinds of power: their dollars, their votes, and their bodies (through disruptive demonstrations). If we began by organizing our dollars, in due time we could use some of our networks to support political action.

At present, with the publication of Al Gore's *Earth in the Balance* and his election to the vice presidency, we have the beginnings of a significant political leadership. It is not yet clear how the churches can connect with and help develop the political forces to provide congressional support for Gore's program. At some point, the environmental thrust of our government needs to change.

In all of this work, there needs to be an empowering community of persons who through action, ritual, and the sharing of deep convictions support and sustain each other. This can be the creation-centered community of the Christian church.

The Calling to Live in Covenant

Our calling is to become a part of a creation community in which the members covenant to care for each other and for the creation. Such a group might work toward affirming and realizing a covenant such as the following:

God, having covenanted with us to be a people for, with, and in communion with all persons and with the planet earth and the universe, we covenant together to be such a people.

We covenant together to seek a way to be free from the alluring addictions of our society—possessions, cars, houses, yachts, clothes, food, alcohol, drugs, completely absorbing work, travel, violence, noise, body development, food—and to be free to care for each other, for the community and its creative institutions, for the entire human community, for the resources of the planet, and for the beauty and life of the natural world.

We covenant together to become aware of the state of the world and of the threats to a sustainable society posed by environmental degradation. We covenant together to find ways to use less of the resources of the world and to develop a lifestyle that might be relevant for all persons everywhere in terms of its drain on resources and its polluting by-products, a lifestyle that may provide deep joys and satisfactions in allowing us to be related to each other in celebration, creative recreational activities, and self-produced entertainment.

We covenant together to share with each other our major decisions, to listen to each other, and to be with each other enough to become real parts of each other.

We covenant together to attend to at least one of the major challenges of our common world for the sake of each other and our God. We further covenant to be responsible to each other—to be responsible stewards in carrying out the tasks of the community or association.

We covenant all this in such a way that we are at once bound together and free to be our deepest selves, the selves we feel called by our God to be.

If a group of persons took this covenant seriously, it would become a kind of anticipation of the future, a foretaste of what we must move toward, a bit of heaven on earth, a beloved community, a creation community that points the way toward a new creation, an embodiment that takes the image of the body of Christ seriously. This kind of action is what the Swiss theologian, Emil Brunner, calls *eschatological action*, action without special regard to its practical consequences. Such action may seem preposterous, romantic, and impossible, but if the churches are to be relevant for a future that is commensurate with the character of their calling, they will move in this direction.

Appendix A

One Hundred Sixty Responses to
What the Natural World Is Telling Us

Citizen Action to Reduce Carbon Dioxide Emissions

1. Recycle everything possible: metals, glass, oil, paper, organic wastes, batteries.

2. Turn off lights. Develop the habit. Reward children and young people for turning off lights. Start a Watt Watchers program in your local schools.

3. Keep refrigerators at thirty-eight to forty-two degrees and freezers at zero to five degrees.

4. Eat no meat or less meat to reduce the amount of fossil fuels used in food production. Six times as much energy is used if you eat beef instead of grain. The same amount of fossil fuel used to provide fertilizer for cattle feed can help produce six times as much grain. Buy locally produced food to eliminate transportation.

5. Buy recycled paper.

6. Buy less. Consume less. Reduce consumption wherever possible, especially of throw-away items.

7. Photocopy on both sides; reuse copy paper when one side is clean.

8. Use mugs or glasses instead of Styrofoam or paper cups.

9. Use rags and handkerchiefs instead of paper products.

10. Dry clothes on racks or clotheslines.

11. Take cloth or net bags to the store for groceries instead of using paper or plastic bags.

12. Reduce or eliminate use of disposables: plastic razors, disposable pens, diapers, pans with cake mixes, plates with TV dinners.

13. Substitute a sweater for more heat.

14. Regulate thermostats; close off unused rooms.

15. Keep fireplace dampers closed except when in use.

16. Insulate water heaters.

17. Replace incandescent light bulbs with fluorescent bulbs, at least in major fixtures.

18. Install automatic shutoffs on lights in rooms little used or used for short periods.

19. Fix leaky faucets immediately.

20. Put reflectors on radiators—cardboard plus tinfoil will do it.

21. Install shower heads that save water and that have a shutoff valve.

22. Clean filters on air conditioners once a month and clean condensers on refrigerators.

23. Use natural gas for heating, where possible, instead of electricity, coal, or oil.

24. Investigate inexpensive sources of energy audits for your home or secure materials and learn how to take an audit. Share audit with friends and neighbors and at public meetings.

25. Have furnace cleaned yearly and inspected for efficiency.

26. Secure electrical efficiency charts for all appliances. Share these charts with others.

27. Plan to drive a car that gets maximum mileage—at least forty miles per gallon—as soon as possible.

28. Investigate mileage of all cars for sale, soon to be produced, and in the prototype stage. Share information with everyone. Post mileage charts in public places.

29. Inform yourself about carbon dioxide emission and its effects on global warming. Commit yourself to reading about the issues.

30. Discuss these issues with institutions to which you are related; ask questions of pastors and business associates.

31. Organize a task force on ecological issues in your church; inform yourself, inform others, post material on bulletin boards.

32. Create and distribute an inventory of energy efficiency for homes and businesses.

33. Consider the possibility of solar energy.

34. Consider how to use trees to shield homes from heat in summer and from wind in winter.

35. Follow legislative action that affects regulation of energy efficiency of cars, electric motors, and all appliances; connect with other groups to write to and meet with legislative representatives to lobby for legislation.

36. Support tax on all fossil fuels, highest on coal.

37. Establish permanent connections with individuals and groups working for responsible practice and policy. Subscribe to publications. Support the budgets of responsible organizations.

38. Organize car pools at work, church, and so forth.

39. Consider use of glazes on windows to let sunlight in and prevent heat from going out.

40. Consider working near where you live.

41. Consider moving to or organizing a community committed to caring for the earth and for all life.

42. Consider working and living where public transportation is available.

43. Help your church care for the creation in theory and in practice.

44. Locate resources that help you and others understand the issues.

45. Plant one or more trees each year.

Citizen Action Regarding Wastes

46. Avoid using chemical pesticides.

47. Investigate the sources of your food where possible. Find sources that buy from farmers who do not use pesticides or chemical fertilizers.

48. Consider growing your own food where this is an option.

49. Set up a buying club to purchase for a group, such as the members of a church, from suppliers of "safe" food.

50. Support legislators who favor strong legislation to encourage the use of alternatives to chemical pesticides and chemical fertilizers.

51. Get lists of toxic home products. See *Save Our Planet: Fifty Simple Things You Can Do To Save the Planet*, pages 40–41.

52. Use nonharmful substitutes for cleaning, such as baking soda or salt for general cleaning, vinegar in water for cleaning glass and tile floors, oil and vinegar for cleaning furniture and wood floors, cloves and citrus oil for flies.

53. Support legislators who push for legislation to ban chlorofluorocarbons and label products now containing them.

54. Repair air conditioners in cars at repair shops that recover chlorofluorocarbons.

55. Help discover, publicize, or create agencies that take old refrigerators and air conditioners to recover and recycle refrigerant and metal.

56. Use fiberglass instead of foam insulation.

57. Avoid purchasing clothes that require dry cleaning, which uses chlorinated solvents, or clean them infrequently.

58. Separate out your toxic products and find ways to dispose of them at sites where they are treated as hazardous wastes.

59. Join with local groups and neighbors to pressure polluting industries to search for productive processes that reduce hazardous wastes.

60. Use less of everything. Repair, borrow, share. Buy what lasts (e.g., rechargeable batteries, fluorescent lights).

61. Buy degradable products—cloth diapers, napkins, handkerchiefs.

62. Use mugs rather than paper cups, paper rather than plastic cups.

63. Buy products in reusable or recyclable containers.

64. Press for reusable standard containers.

65. Do not use juices, cakes, or microwavable foods in throwaway containers or pans.

66. Buy products with less packaging. Leave extra stuff with seller.

67. Buy products in bulk where possible—tea, for example.

68. Procure or make cloth or string bags for groceries.

69. Buy nontoxic detergents.

70. Save paper by photocopying on both sides.

71. Buy recycled products, paper, toilet paper, and so forth.

72. Do not buy throwaway products—plastic razors, pens, and so on.

73. Separate all wastes and recycle metals, class, paper, plastics, batteries, oil, and tires.

74. Organize recycling in your home, office, church, school, club.

75. Compost organic wastes, including lawn trimmings, or find a neighbor who is; take organic wastes to composting center or organize such a center.

76. Stop junk mail by writing to Mail Preference Service, Direct Marketing Association, 11 West 42nd St., P.O. Box 3861, New York, NY 10163-3861.

Citizen Action Regarding the Developing World Economy

77. Support anything that we can do to reduce carbon emissions and to increase the number of trees taking carbon out of the air. This will pro-

vide some room for the developing world economy and also might provide a more relevant pattern for the developing world to emulate.

78. Similarly, support anything that we can do to reduce ozone depletion. This will provide more space for the developing world economy and should lead to alternative technologies useful in the developing world.

79. Support financially and participate in organizations that care for the environment, such as the Natural Resources Defense Council, Bread for the World, and the Worldwatch Institute.

80. Begin to transform your way of being so that the way you live can be relevant for all people—that is, live so that what you do can be universalized without disastrous consequences.

81. If you have money to invest, examine the policies of corporations with regard to any number of issues, including environmental issues.

82. Organize a Care for the Creation Task Force in your church to write a policy statement that can become the basis for actions individually and collectively. Secure commitment from members to attend to what is going on in one developing country. Choose a country for yourself.

83. Seriously consider with others the possibility of transforming the place where you live into a place where you can begin to live in a way that is relevant for the future—that is, a way that is sustainable locally, nationally, and internationally.

84. Examine educational material that might be useful in church school and in local schools. Find a way to influence the content of education.

Citizen Action Regarding Ozone Depletion

85. Only purchase aerosol products that do not use chlorofluorocarbons.

86. Do not use Styrofoam products: drinking cups, picnic coolers, packing materials, or insulation. Non-CFC foam insulation is available.

87. Do not buy halon fire extinguishers having bromine contents.

88. When your air conditioner needs attention, get it fixed immediately at a repair establishment that has a policy of collecting and recycling the CFC coolant.

89. Join an environmental group working to secure governmental action to ban use of CFCs. Participate in campaigns to bring the issue to the attention of your congressperson.

90. Help initiate programs of education in churches, schools, clubs.

Citizen Action in the Area of Economic Theory and Practice

91. Join with others to secure newspaper, radio, and television coverage of the issues.

92. Support action to get local governments to collect and recycle refrigerators and air conditioners.

93. Secure educational materials at several different levels to educate yourself and to distribute to friends and colleagues.

94. Put a substantial amount in your personal budget to support organizations and to buy materials to have them available for distribution at the drop of a hat.

Citizen Action Regarding Water

95. Install aerated faucets. About one gallon of water per day would be saved by every American if all faucets had such aerators.

96. Use special shower heads that use little water and have a shutoff at the head.

97. Put plastic bottles filled with water in toilet tanks, install special low-water-use mechanisms, or install a dam.

98. Wash car with buckets rather than hose or at self-service wash station.

99. Do not use running water to wash hands or dishes or to shave—fill bowl instead.

100. Fix leaky faucets immediately.

101. If you use water for lawns and gardens, consider a system that collects water from laundry, sink, and shower and makes it available for re-cycling.

102. Become acquainted with water issues and participate in town, city, state, and national decision-making processes regarding disposal of garbage, processing of sewage, and ways to use water efficiently, such as limits on sprinkling. Push for the allocation of resources to the EPA to initiate and monitor water and the industrial processes that pollute it.

103. Run clothes washer and dishwashers only when full.

104. Water plants with rainwater.

105. Store cold water in the refrigerator for drinking.

106. Take showers rather than baths.

107. Find a way to test your water for toxic materials or find someone who can test it.

Citizen Action in the Area of Economic Theory and Practice

108. Examine the policies of companies whose products you buy. Read *Shopping for a Better World*, published by CEP, and *Rating American Corporate Conscience*, published by Addison-Wesley. Join CEP (Council for Economic Priorities) by writing 30 Irving Place, New York, NY 10003.

109. Distribute copies of *Shopping for a Better World.*

110. Secure the list of Green committees of correspondence in your community from Green Committees of Correspondence Clearinghouse, P.O. Box 30208, Kansas City, MO 64112. Explore their programs. Secure information through them about local institutions and their programs to be responsible ecologically. Join with them to pressure organizations for more responsibility.

111. Secure from organizations such as the Natural Resources Defense Council information regarding corporations that are especially guilty of corporate irresponsibility toward the environment. Support such organizations. Write to the Natural Resources Defense Council, 40 West 20th St., New York, NY 10011.

112. Read *For the Common Good* by Herman Daly and John Cobb (Beacon Press) and organize a study group to discuss the book. Read chapters in the following order: 19, 20, 11–18, 1–10.

113. Read M. Douglas Meeks, *God the Economist* (Fortress Press).

114. Opt out of high-consumption patterns of living; buy less, budget expenditures, establish a policy of consultation with a spouse or a significant friend who is sympathetic to the direction of your thinking before any expenditure of over ten dollars except for food. Put *Living More with Less,* by Doris Janzen Longacre, beside your bed, along with the Bible. Also consult *99 Ways to a Simple Lifestyle,* from the Center for Science in the Public Interest.

115. Examine your work situation, preferably in a group concerned with such issues, hopefully in your congregation. Are you producing and promoting something "essential" to meet basic human needs? Consider changing jobs if your situation is not satisfactory.

116. Consider how you can raise questions about the excessive consumption of our society.

117. Develop a covenant to protect the environment with your congregation or with a special group of friends.

118. Participate in or organize a Care for the Creation Task Force in your congregation.

119. Develop a network of services and resources in which persons will be willing to trade what they have or can do for what others have or can do—an alternative exchange system. Develop an inventory of skills. (One church built its own new addition using such a network.)

120. Establish a system of recognition for those who find creative ways to reduce consumption. Share discoveries with each other.

121. Organize recreational events in the congregation, thus reducing the need to purchase recreation. Include drama and other activities that encourage participation and personal development.

122. Introduce educational materials on simpler lifestyles in church school classes.

123. Examine the resources in your community for organically produced foods. Examine the policies of institutions with which you are connected for purchase of organically produced foods. Organize groups to pressure stores to stock such foods. Provide information about sources for organically produced foods. Inform yourself about pesticides. Consult farm bureaus and agricultural agents.

124. Consider producing your own food. Secure resources from *Ecology Action,* 5798 Ridgewood Road, Willits, CA 95490. Consult *The Green Consumer* (pages 77–134), "Food and Groceries" in *Green Lifestyle Handbook* (pages 93–104), and *EarthRight* (pages 1–38).

125. Examine your investment policies in light of suggestions from Susan Meeker Lowry, *Economics as if the Earth Really Mattered: A Catalyst Guide to Socially Conscious Investing,* New Society Publishers, P.O. Box 582, Santa Cruz, CA 95061.

126. Support Bread for the World, 802 Rhode Island Ave. NE, Washington, D.C. 20077-5204.

127. Join, support, and participate in the Green committees of correspondence. Contact the Green Committees of Correspondence Clearinghouse, P.O. Box 30208, Kansas City, MO 64112. Secure a list of committees in your part of the country from the clearinghouse.

128. Take time to appreciate and realize that whatever you do that moves in the direction of caring for the creation will be of some ultimate meaning and significance in the economy of God.

Citizen Action Regarding the Population Explosion

129. Make copies of this list and distribute them widely.

130. Read Paul and Anne Ehrlich, *Population Explosion.*

131. Organize a study group in your church to discuss this issue along with other environmental issues.

132. Arrange for showings of the ten videos in the series "Race to Save the Planet."

133. Join the Green movement. Contact Green Committees of Correspondence Clearinghouse, P.O. Box 30208, Kansas City, MO 64112.

134. Read John Robbins, *Diet for a New America.*

135. Save the resources used for the production of meat by not eating meat, at least not grain-fed animals.

136. As soon as you have a few persons who are informed about the issues, arrange meetings with congresspersons and also with all the media to encourage programs on the population explosion. These persons may be discovered and even produced by your educational activities.

137. Begin to develop a library of resources on the issues.

138. Contact teachers in your schools to encourage units on the population explosion.

139. Sponsor essay contests in the schools.

140. Discover and promote speakers in churches, schools, clubs, and so forth.

141. Choose one of the developing countries to study and understand what is happening in the country on this issue as well as others. Become informed—become related to the reality of population explosion.

142. Hold a discussion on the implications of the population explosion for the population growth in the United States. Are there implications for reproduction as a Christian directive?

Citizen Action Regarding Global Citizenship

143. Read daily Matt. 25:31–46.

144. Learn about one of the poorer countries of the world.

145. With the help of your denominational mission board, choose a church involved with the poorer persons of the country of your choice. Write the minister and ask for the name of a person with whom to correspond, maybe specifying some knowledge of English, maybe not. Begin to correspond. Begin to learn the language if you do not already know it.

146. Begin to make plans to visit the country and live with or near the person or persons involved for at least ten days.

147. Begin to make plans to establish a sister church relationship with a church in the country. Encourage others in the church to relate to somebody in the sister church. Involve young people in the relationship.

148. Find some books that describe how the United States is involved with the country. Think about finding a course somewhere that deals with the country.

149. Consider how you might invite your correspondent and maybe others (perhaps the pastor of the church) to visit you.

150. Begin to seek ways to be of some help in the work of the sister church.

151. Hopefully, some nationals from the country will be living nearby where you can relate to them and what is happening to them in the United States.

152. Hopefully, these persons will be related to a church that can be a sister church for your church. If not, find a church, of your denomination preferably, that is in a disadvantaged area. Begin to relate to the church, perhaps offering to do something in the context of its ordinary life, like teach church school or work with youth groups. Language proficiency is crucial here.

153. Understand all of this as being an opportunity for you to minister to persons whose location in life may be quite different from yours and yet, at a deeper level, the same.

154. Understand that you are responsible for the disastrous poverty of persons locally and internationally because you participate in and support the functioning of our economic, political, and military forces around the world.

155. Pray daily that you will be able to understand how what happens to others happens to you and what happens to you happens to others.

156. Be open to the possibility that this can be the richest, most meaningful experience of your life. Let the Spirit lead you. Throw away your preconceived ideas about other persons.

157. Be aware that all of these suggestions may simply get in the way of your own leading by the Spirit to something meaningful.

158. Meet regularly with others involved in this direction of church life.

159. Read 1 Cor. 12:12–26.

160. Be aware that environmental issues can absorb you and make you obnoxious to the rest of the people of God.

Appendix B

Nine Reasons to Eat Less Meat

I stopped eating meat in September of 1989 because I read in John Robbins's book *Diet for a New America* that it would save a lot of grain—twelve million tons per year, it was asserted. I continue not to eat meat because it seems to me that it was costing the rest of the world too much for me to eat meat—water and air pollution, loss of topsoil, tropical forests burned for cattle growing. I am convinced that we should consume much less, including much less meat. I know that there are a number of health reasons for not eating meat, but here I concentrate on other reasons.

1. We could use the grain that we feed livestock to provide food in the form of grain for more people—five times as many, some claim. The latest figures from the Department of Agriculture, as reported in *Worldwatch* magazine for May–June 1991, indicate that it takes 6.9 pounds of grain on the average to produce 1 pound of pork, 4.8 pounds of grain to produce 1 pound of beef, 2.8 pounds of grain to produce 1 pound of chicken, and 2.6 pounds of grain to produce 1 pound of eggs. While these figures are considerably better than the figures quoted in *Diet for a New America,* it still means that many more persons could be fed by the grain now fed to animals. I am very aware of the difficulty of providing food for the hungry of the world. Giving food in the form of aid is very complicated and involves the consideration of such actions on the markets of the world and on the incentives of the poorer nations' peoples to produce for themselves. Nevertheless, one thing is clear: there is no conceiv-

able way for the five billion persons living today to eat the way we do in the United States, even if they had the money.

2. The pressure on the land used to grow the extra grain used to produce meat contributes to the degradation of land. More land is used, poorer land is used, and grazing and growth patterns leave the land with less topsoil and push farmers into using chemical fertilizers and pesticides to meet the demand for meat. Public lands are overgrazed. Forty percent of the world's grain and 70 percent of U.S. production was used for livestock in 1990, a total of 262 million tons. The degradation of the land leaves us less able to meet the food needs of the future. Four million acres of cropland are said to be lost each year due to erosion. Much of this loss must be attributed to the pressures caused by livestock raising.

3. The pressure to provide the grain for livestock is one of the causes of the destruction of forests both at home and in Central and South America. The destruction of forests not only leads to soil erosion but also to the increase of carbon dioxide in the atmosphere, because trees use considerable carbon dioxide in their growing. The increase in carbon dioxide leads to global warming, the consequences of which may be catastrophic in the years ahead. Costa Rica, for example, has lost 83 percent of its forests; Brazil, about 50 percent. While no one would claim that all of this loss is due to our meat-eating habits, a part of it is. Some experts claim that we lose forty-five square feet of Central American forest for every hamburger we produce from their cattle.

4. The destruction of the tropical forests also destroys millions of plant species. Costa Rica once had 5 percent of the plant species in the world.

5. The energy used in the production of food to feed livestock uses up our fossil fuels both to run the machines and to produce the fertilizers used in agriculture. Fourteen thousand kilocalories are required, some report, to produce a pound of pork, the equivalent of about one-half gallon of gasoline. On the average, the energy used per person to produce pork, beef, and poultry is equal to fifty gallons of gasoline per year. Vegetarian diets require one-third the energy.

6. The use of the energy equivalent of fifty gallons of gasoline means the emission of about 1,000 pounds of carbon dioxide, a greenhouse gas that is the chief cause of global warming. That means 666 more pounds of carbon dioxide than if one were on a vegetarian diet. The diets of 250 million persons thus cause the emission of over 88 million more tons of carbon dioxide than would be produced by persons with vegetarian diets. There are those who say that we must cut our total carbon dioxide emis-

sions by at least 75 percent. This would leave us with total emissions from all sectors (industry, electricity production, and transportation) of about 375 million tons. Saving 88 million tons of carbon dioxide thus seems like a necessary move.

7. Producing the extra grain to feed livestock instead of using it to feed persons uses all kinds of resources, especially water. One pound of pork uses 430 gallons of water; one pound of beef, 390 gallons; one pound of chicken, 375 gallons. It is obvious that it takes as much more water as it takes more grain, roughly five times as much on the average. Water is in short supply in many places and is procured only by lowering the water levels in underground aquifers. Thus, the water used to produce meat averages about 190 gallons per person per year, or twice what a typical American uses at home for all purposes. In the Pacific Northwest, it is estimated that the water saved from irrigation for livestock feeding would produce seventeen billion kilowatt hours of energy a year.

8. The livestock industry produces tons of waste. Three-quarters of this waste is taken care of by natural decomposition, but the other one-quarter from feedlots and chicken factories must be disposed of while protecting water resources. There is much debate as to how responsible the industry is. The *Worldwatch* May–June 1991 article "Fat of the Land" reports that the Chesapeake Bay contains evidence of manure as a source of the nitrogen and phosphorous that overfertilize algae and disturb the aquatic ecosystem. One estimate puts the contribution of animals wastes at 40 percent of the nitrogen and 35 percent of the phosphorous in our water systems. Even where the wastes are deposited in fields, the wastes can pollute wells and water supplies.

9. In addition, cattle, goats, and sheep expel methane, which is another greenhouse gas. For each pound of beef, the atmosphere receives about one-third of a pound of methane.

One might continue to argue for giving up meat because of the direct effect of eating meat on our health. I will not do this. Suffice it to say that it simply costs the world too much for us to eat meat. One can debate just how much it costs the world to eat different kinds of meat, especially fish. In the meantime, it makes sense to stop eating meat except for fish. There is no way for the rest of the world to move toward our diet of meat without aiding in the destruction of our natural life-support systems.

Appendix C

Sixteen Reasons to Recycle

The earth is crying out to us to care for it, to use its resources carefully—to reduce consumption, to reuse, and to recycle. The creation and the Creator are groaning because of the way we are destroying the earth. Thus, we should recycle for the following reasons:

1. To reduce the amount of garbage and slow down the filling up of landfills.

2. To reduce the cost of garbage disposal.

3. To recycle is to reduce the amount of energy used in the production of aluminum, steel, glass, and paper products: about 90 percent for aluminum, about 70 percent for steel, about 30 percent for glass, and from 30 to 55 percent for paper.

4. To reduce carbon emissions, thus postponing the effects of global warming.

5. To reduce the cost of production.

6. To reduce the amount of water used in the production process and thus to reduce the costs, the shortfall of water, and the amount of water that is disposed of in the production process. One ton of recycled steel saves twenty-five tons of water, some estimate.

7. To reduce the wastes that are part of the ordinary production process for raw materials. One ton of recycled steel prevents two hundred pounds of air pollutants, one hundred pounds of water pollutants, and three tons of mining wastes, according to some estimates.

8. To reduce the amount of toxic chemicals used in the production process and to reduce the toxins given off in the disposal of water.

9. To reduce the number of trees used in the production process. The unharvested trees continue to use carbon dioxide in photosynthesis, thus slowing global warming. Some estimate that paper mills can reduce air pollution 74 percent by using waste paper rather than virgin pulp.

10. To reduce the need to cut down the trees that prevent water run-offs, floods, and the erosion of soils.

11. To help slow down the depletion of nonrenewable minerals. Recycling one ton of aluminum eliminates the need for four tons of bauxite and almost one ton of petroleum coke and pitch, say researchers.

12. To provide jobs in the recycling industry, more jobs than are available in the process of providing raw materials.

13. To call attention to our consumption habits and the possibility and worth of consuming less.

14. To call attention to the wastes involved in packaging and in many other areas of the production-consumption-disposal cycle.

15. To call attention to the usefulness of quality purchasing.

16. To provide many persons, young and old, with an activity that is useful and meaningful. It may help one feel related to the creation and the Creator.

Appendix D

Twelve Reasons to Buy Less

1. If we buy less, we will save energy. Everything we buy, including food, uses energy in the production process. Energy comes almost entirely from fossil fuels, the burning of which produces carbon dioxide, smog, and acid rain.

2. If we buy less, we will help save both fuel and nonfuel resources for future generations. If we continue to use oil and natural gas at the present rates, experts predict that the world will run out of oil in somewhere between 50 and 100 years and out of natural gas in somewhere between 120 and 200 years. In addition, almost everything that we buy uses nonfuel minerals in one way or another. Many are in short supply.

3. If we buy less, we will put less pressure on our corporations to exploit Third World countries for the resources needed in production. It will also put less pressure on our government to use its political, economic, and military powers to keep these resources flowing. Third World countries then would be freer to produce life-support crops for their own people and to put less pressure on their institutions to open up tropical forests to grow crops.

4. If we buy less, we will save the money it costs to dispose of garbage and save ourselves from burying ourselves in it. Everything we buy must, in one form or another, go back into the earth or into the air. A useful principle is to produce only the amount that can be absorbed or repro-

cessed by the earth or the atmosphere. We are running out of space, according to some; others say that if we pay enough, some persons will permit their space to be used. It is clear that we are producing stuff that cannot be reprocessed in measurable amounts of time—radioactive substances and plastics, for example. We might be much better off to produce things that last longer, thus not requiring replacement so often. We should also resist all pressures to create artificial obsolescence, to use techniques such as changes in style to make things useless psychologically even when they are useful physically. Style changes and status advertisements must be viewed as essentially destructive of the creation.

5. If we buy less, we may need to work less; it may reduce the pressure on us to work more to have more. Thus, we could reorder economic life in the direction of a thirty-hour week, giving us more time to live in relationship with each other.

6. If we buy less, we may find other ways of filling our time and finding meaning. We must admit that buying often fills the vacuum of meaning in our lives. Buying can be understood as a way of avoiding finding something significant to be about.

7. If we buy less, we may be healthier. Some 60 percent of U.S. women and 50 percent of U.S. men are said to have health problems because they are overweight. This consumption of unneeded food uses extra fertilizer, which results in more pollution of groundwater; the extra pesticides required threaten our health as they seep into the groundwater. The extra energy required contributes to carbon dioxide emissions and global-warming threats. The extra water required contributes to our water shortages, actual and threatened.

8. If we buy less, it may be possible to work out ways for those without much to have more. How can we use the money we don't spend and the time we don't need to spend in earning a living to help in reordering the redistribution of the world's resources? Twenty percent of U.S. persons live in poverty, and 1.2 billion people in the world live without basic amounts of food, clothing, and shelter. About 12 million people, mostly children under age five, die from hunger and hunger-related diseases every year.

9. If we buy less, we may find a way of being that brings more joy into our lives as we feel ourselves more connected to others and to the creation.

10. If we buy less, we may feel that we are more in harmony with the underlying realities and movements of the universe—with what we designate as God.

11. If we buy less, it may help someone else decide to buy less.

12. If we buy less, we may have more time to be for, with, and in communion with our families, our friends, our sisters and brothers everywhere, our world, and our God.

Appendix E

University Church: Care for the Creation Inventory

The Inventory Group of University Church, Chicago, used locations around the church to focus on ways to think about environmental responsibility in relation to the building and the congregational life.

Kitchen and Dining Room

1. Lights: What kind of lights do we have? Are they efficient in the use of electricity? Could we make do with less? Automatic turnoffs? Can we use fluorescent bulbs with dimmers? Change the dimmers? Use reflectors to increase the effectiveness of lights?

2. Refrigerator: Is ours efficient? How do we dispose of the old unused one so that chlorofluorocarbons are recycled? It is already or soon will be illegal to dump refrigerators in the alley without proper disposal of the coolant.

3. Stove: Check height of pilot.

4. Trash: Should there be bins in all offices to separate recyclables? Consultation with all nonchurch agencies that use space for offices? Workshop on how to separate paper? Is there any way to compost from church suppers and so forth?

5. Windows: Windows seem leaky. Caulking? Storm windows?

6. Temperature: Is there a separate thermostat for this area? Is there control for unused times?

7. Hot water: Would a dishwasher save water? Have we monitored

the times when hot water is needed, or do we keep water hot enough to meet standards all the time?

8. Washing dishes: Are we wasting water by using huge sink tubs to wash dishes? Dishpan substitute?

9. Is there any attempt to advocate nonmeat dishes at potlucks and at other meals served on various occasions? Should we help by providing recipes? Promotion of vegetarian menus?

Library

1. Windows: Need attention. Storms?

2. Fireplace: Flue stuffed?

3. Lighting: Fluorescent? Automatic timer, especially for use during the week?

4. Radiators: More efficient by use of reflectors? Efficiency vents or valves?

5. Books and other source materials: Environmental library, including books, magazines, catalogues of products? Should we supply books and so forth for sale? Light bulbs and other gadgets, such as aerated faucets, shower heads, toilet-water-saving devices? Should we publicize sources for such materials if we cannot provide space and purchasing opportunities? Sunday morning displays, sales? Should we cosponsor an environment center at another site?

Sanctuary

1. Thermostat: Requirements of the organ for heat?

2. Fans: Evidence is inconclusive about their usefulness for large spaces. Is it worth investigating?

3. Lights: What kind of bulbs? Substantial cost to get scaffolding to change bulbs? Prepare for major change when replacements are necessary. Small table lamps instead of overhead lights now used?

4. Fireplace: Check flue.

Office

1. Paper: Purchase recycled paper? Purchasing policy? Statement of policy. Sign on all publications.

2. Photocopies: Double-sided photocopy? Reuse of paper printed on one side? Messages on half sheets?

Building in General

1. Audit: Hire a consultant to do energy audit, including functioning of the furnace, insulation of roof, and so on.

2. Cleaning: Use of environmentally friendly chemicals for cleaning?

3. Worship: How to make environmental issues relevant in our worship? Call to worship, prayers, hymns, liturgical dance, symbols in sanctuary, earth flag, affirmations, benedictions, sermons, announcements in bulletin, bulletin cover. Are we collecting materials to have files available for participants? Use of special-emphasis Sundays. How to handle resistance to so-called unspiritual interpretation of environmental issues? Need for theological interpretation of the issues.

Church Program

1. Christian development: Are there church school units on the creation and environmental issues at all levels? Is there any discussion of how church members can be involved in school, home, community, business, politics? Are there pictures, symbols, materials on classroom walls that indicate the dimensions involved in thinking about the creation and environmental issues? Is everything done with a view toward proportion, taking into account the variety of persons and interests in the congregation and the perceived need at this time of a special focus on the environment?

2. Bulletin boards, walls, and halls: Is there material displayed attractively, frequently changed, and easily read, including the small print?

3. Connections with other churches and church bodies: Are we effective in connecting to and providing leadership in the wider church?

4. Connections with other organizations: Are the church members active in other environmental organizations? Do they provide information and access to community events? Is there a regular way of processing these events and publicizing relevant ones?

5. Task Force: Do we have an active task force focused on listening to and caring for the creation? Have we provided information for our church as a whole about what is going on in the task force?

Appendix F

The Riverside Church Declaration on
the Earth Community and Ecological Stewardship:
Becoming an Earth Community Congregation*

Preamble

1. The peril facing the planet and the earth community is not only the possibility of the destruction of life forms by nuclear war. It is also the more important peril of the slow degradation and destruction of life forms, life systems, planetary cycles, and energy flows.

2. As the Riverside Church in the late 1970s gave leadership through its Disarmament Program, it now desires to respond creatively to the planetary peril of ecological degradation and destruction in the crucial decade of the 1990s, considered by some as the "Decade of Decisions."

3. The Riverside Church acknowledges the efforts of thousands of secular organizations and governmental institutions the world over that have contributed to the development of an emerging ecological ethos. In the general absences of leadership by religious institutions of ecologically vibrant values, attitudes, spiritualities, and theologies, those organizations have set out to develop their own ecological ethos.

4. In particular, Riverside recognizes the United Nations Environ-

---

*As of publication, this draft statement by the Riverside Ecology Task Force has not been adopted by the church council or by the congregation.

mental Programme's leadership and the ecological principles of its World Character for Nature, adopted by the UN General Assembly in 1986, by whose "principles of conservation . . . all human conduct affecting nature is to be guided and judged." It also acknowledges the valiant efforts of the World Commission on Environment, whose highly acclaimed 1987 report, "Our Common Future," called "for a common endeavor and for new norms of behavior at all levels and in the interest of all." Riverside considers these activities during the last two decades to be major contributions to the development of ecological norms and values. We are committed to their further development.

5. In the interest of the members of the earth community—including the living planet or Gaia itself—the Riverside Church, after searching its spirit and the spirit of the earth community, declares and affirms within its own religious framework its religious role in that earth community. This framework includes its Judeo-Christian values and traditions and the religious and cultural values of other societies. A functional cosmology based upon scientific achievements in paleontology, astronomy, astrophysics, comparative history of cultures, etc., is also considered to form an essential component of its ecologically sensitive religious framework.

6. The following Declarations (containing statements of analysis) and Affirmations (containing statements of resolve) form a statement of Riverside's present religiously inspired ecological consciousness and commitment.

Declarations

1. The Riverside Church declares that no genuine spirituality is possible in our emergent ecological age without the inclusion of a "functional cosmology," i.e., a scientifically based attempt to explain creation, evolution, and the present structure and direction of the universe.

2. The Riverside Church declares that part of a needed functional cosmology is the belief that we are part of and in union with all life forms and with all the earth. Riverside Church questions the uncritical view of the universe which holds humankind as its central fact and purpose. This belief has come to characterize the scientific-technological age in which we are now living.

3. The Riverside Church declares that within this earth-centered orientation to the emerging ecological age, it wants to continue to steadfastly work for justice and peace. It declares that its ecological vision includes a strong commitment to global justice, which reduces the main

causes of ecological degradation, i.e., gross affluence and gross impoverishment within and between nations.

4. The Riverside Church declares that in its pursuit of being a responsible part of the Earth Community, it will develop a "spirituality of the Earth Community" that will be based upon a wide array of revelatory resources. This spirituality will include its own biblical affirmation, "The Earth is the Lord's," as well as those that deal with care of the earth, God's covenant with the planet's people, and stewardship of the Earth's resources. It will also incorporate in the rebuilding of its creation-centered spirituality the writings of medieval mystics such as Master Eckhardt, Julian Hildegard, and the insights and practices of other scriptural and non-scriptural religions and value systems. In particular, it will search for appropriate values and symbols in the religious biocentrism of native Americans in North, Central, and South American countries.

5. The Riverside Church declares that the economic dimensions of its ecological spirituality with its associated practice of ecological stewardship has to include the following ingredients: a) maintenance of the inseparable ecological trinity of economics, environment, and energy; b) appropriate, self-reliant socioeconomic development, particularly in the agricultural sector; c) reduction of the maldistribution of resources inside and between the industrialized, pastoral, nomadic, and agricultural societies. Ecological justice, or ecojustice, demands the Earth's bounty be shared among humans and between humans and other living beings in the Earth Community. Commitment to a simple, frugal lifestyle makes this possible.

6. The Riverside Church declares that the cultural dimension of its ecological spirituality and its associated practice of ecological stewardship has to include the following ingredients: a) a substantial shift away from an excessively anthropocentric culture with characteristics of materialism, consumerism, competitiveness, aggression, etc., to a culture in which care of the planet and its life is central or dominant (ecocentrism or ecoarchy); b) nondiscrimination of humans on account of sex, race, or religion, which means, among other things, the reduction of male dominance or patriarchy, both in the interpretation of holy scriptures and in present patriarchal institutions such as multinational corporations, national states, and ecclesiastical institutions.

7. The Riverside Church declares that the political dimension of its ecological spirituality and its associated practice of ecological stewardship within the Earth Community has to include the following ingredients: a) the organization of our planet and its community in an ecologically and

ethically sound way, i.e., according to a political philosophy or organizing principle that places at its center the well-being of the whole Earth Community; b) the organization of societies and communities according to the inseparable unity of economics, environment, and energy, with justice and harmony among all the human and other living beings in the Earth Community; c) reduced political tension and the threat of war among nations because of the unsustainable planetary perils they cause to billions of human beings and trillions of animals and plants; d) respect, demilitarization, depollution, and internationalization of the commons of space with its extraterrestrial resources based upon the rights of everyone in the Earth Community and supported by an international interspecies legal system.

Affirmations

1. The Riverside Church affirms and pledges to become an Earth Community Congregation. It will consider adding a separate "Earth Stewardship Commission" to its present organizational structure; it also affirms and pledges to assist other congregations to become members of a worldwide registry of Earth Community Congregations. This registry, maintained by the International Network for Religion and Ecology, will be part of similar registries for Earth Community Colleges, Earth Community Schools, etc.

2. The Riverside Church affirms and pledges that it, as an Earth Community Congregation, will develop an ecological spirituality and its praxis of ecological stewardship.

3. The Riverside Church affirms and pledges that the following are to be part of its ecological activities:

Inside the Church

a) Encouraging an earth-centered spirituality: an annual series of seminars/workshops; celebrating an Earth Community Liturgy could coincide with the Environmental Sabbath or Holy Day celebration sponsored by the United Nations Environmental Programme; placing in the center of the chancel a symbol of the Earth Community such as an earth flag with the words "Earth Community Congregation"; revise the church school's curricula within Riverside' ecological spirituality and its praxis of ecological stewardship; providing information activities including a special Ecological Resources Information Center in the church library, tabling, a permanent bulletin board; engaging in extensive networking with religious ecological groups; promoting the development of a lifestyle of voluntary simplicity; urging church members to consider eating low on the food chain; taking leadership in establishing one or more food cooperatives that carry locally and organically produced foods for competitive prices. b) Increasing energy efficiency: conducting periodic energy audits, including a feasibility study with Union Seminary and the Interchurch Center; implementing of cost-effective energy-efficiency measures; helping to establish an interfaith council on energy to reduce energy costs and promote energy efficiency in metropolitan religious institutions. c) Increasing resource efficiency: reduction of paper, use of both sides of the page and of recycled paper by all church offices; prohibiting environmentally unsound materials, Styrofoam cups; reduction of plastic in cafeteria operation; investing in corporations that build up rather than damage the environment, particularly those that subscribe to the recently formulated Valdez principles. d) Increasing recycling, reuse, and reduction: collaborating, to the greatest extent, with existing programs; participating at the neighborhood recycling program at the Cathedral of St. John the Divine and urging its expansion into domestic chemical waste, particularly batteries; organizing workshops for reuse of materials; considering the feasibility of establishing a Community Technology Center that would help church members and local residents to be more self-reliant technically, assisting them in reusing materials, and providing them with information on the political, economic, and cultural aspects of ecological stewardship and the political philosophy of environmentalism. e) Regenerating the earth and its life-support systems: combatting air, land, water, and ocean pollution by having church members join local organizations such as the North River Waste Water Treatment Review Board and by planting a dozen trees around the church perimeter and engaging in flower gardening in containers.

4. The Riverside Church affirms and pledges to engage in the following ecological outreach activities:

Outside the Riverside Church within the Religious Community

a) Attempt to organize for the next five to ten years two major annual events: 1) a Fall consultation of about 40 church leaders, theologians, scientists, and community activists, leading to a practical program of work; 2) a Spring conference to communicate this program of work to churches at large. It would attempt to include intellectual and spiritual leaders of Columbia University, Union Theological Seminary, Jewish Theological Seminary, the Interchurch Center, the Cathedral of St. John the Divine, and the Manhattan School of Music, all located within one square mile of the church. b) Work diligently in developing ecological liturgies and symbols that can be used by other churches, particularly for the Environmental Sabbath around June 5, World Environment Day. It may possibly develop into an Earth Community Symbol Liturgy that would substitute the Earth Community flag in churches for an American flag or symbol, thus emphasizing the prophetic character of the church, both in ecological and nonecological matters. c) Help other churches to declare themselves Earth Community Congregations by sharing its experience in their congregation-wide process of determining their role in their bioregions. d) Be at the service of Riverside's constituent denominations and their mission boards for participation in overseas partner church programs of ecological stewardship such as the development of bioregionally appropriate spiritualities of the Earth Community and their associate praxis of ecological stewardship.

In the Secular Communities

a) Play a prophetic role in the environmental movement by affirming the good accomplished and by kindly and humbly pointing to shortcomings in both governmental and voluntary environmental projects, programs, and policies by letter-writing campaigns, testimony, etc. b) Have its task force on Ecological Stewardship engage in legislative work at local, state, national, and international levels using its informed religious perspective and stressing the need for educational policies that would strengthen the well-being of all members of the Earth Community. c) Have its Ecology Task Force endorse and promote the ten principles of ecological security proposed by the Soviet-American Forum for Life and Rights in September 1989. d) Encourage individual church members to become signatories to the Earth Covenant and have their friends, colleagues, etc., become signatories as well. e) Encourage individual church members to become involved in the development of a political philosophy of environmentalism by taking leadership in the Green movement and networking with the U.S. Committee of Correspondence. f) Have individual church members work for appointment of environmentalists on Environmental Committees of New York City's 69 Community District Boards and other elective and nonelective positions on city, state, and national levels. g) Encourage individual church members to increase their contributions to their chosen environmental organizations, particularly in respect to values clarification and the development of ecologically and cosmologically sensitive lifestyles.

Appendix G

Holden Village Care for the Creation Statement

This is a statement of the Holden Village Task Force on Caring for the Creation, setting forth its view of what Holden's mission might be in this area. It does not represent a consensus of the Holden Village Board or of the long-term community. It is offered as a starting point for local church groups to think about their mission.

Holden Village Task Force, 1989–1990
Caring for the Creation
"The Earth is God's and the Fullness Thereof"

The creation as earth is spectacularly beautiful and incredibly rich in resources. It is being threatened by a lifestyle that results in massive exploitation of unrenewable global resources, in massive global pollution, and in irreversible changes in the nurturing rhythms of the natural world.

We are convinced that these exploitative actions, if not interrupted and significantly altered, will inevitably lead to the inability of the earth to support its present richness and diversity of life, including in its early victims even human beings.

We are further convinced that all earthly life is interdependent and interconnected. Not wishing to be known as the generation that was blind and focused only on serving ourselves, we have entered into a covenant with God and with each other to change our own lives and to work for the recognition of the deep trouble ahead of us unless there are fundamental changes in what we live for and in how we live.

To that end we accept personal responsibility for our continuing part in destroying the earth's capacity to nourish and to nurture, and we are acting together and individually

1. To change our own lifestyles,

2. To heighten awareness of the issues,

3. To collect and disseminate pertinent data,

4. To provide planning assistance for concerned groups, especially churches, with special concern for Lutheran churches,

5. To network with agencies,

6. To provide models by our own individual and institutional behavior,

7. To publish helpful materials in response to the challenge,

8. To register our dismay and opposition to institutions, businesses, governmental agencies, churches and nations—whose actions in our judgment indicate disregard of responsible concern for the creation,

9. To relate to and support other individuals in churches, clubs, places of work, schools, and communities working in helpful directions regarding the environment,

10. To assign a portion of our individual budgets in support of all of this mission.

Appendix H

Ecclesiology and Creation Communities

The most extensive guide to the sources of church and synagogue publications on the environment is the "Guide to Environmental Activities and Resources in the North American Religious Community," published by the Joint Appeal by Religion and Science for the Environment, 1047 Amsterdam Avenue, New York, NY 10025, 212/316-7441.

Another resource guide is "The Whole Earth Church, A Resource Guide," available from David Fergeson, 70A, Devon Court, #3, Edwardsville, IL 62025, 618/656-0502.

A useful workbook that focuses on household opportunities and on building a group is "Household Ecoteam Workbook" from Global Action Plan, 84 Yerry Hill Road, Woodstock, NY 12498.

Further information is available in "Shalom Connections in Personal and Congregational Life" from Program Agency Presbyterian Church, USA, 100 Witherspoon St., Louisville, KY 40202-1396, 502/569-5809.

For information about religious resources, write or call the following organizations:

United Church of Christ, UCC Office for Church in Society, 700 Prospect Avenue East, Cleveland, OH 44115-1100, 216/736-2174.

Mennonite Central Committee, 110 Maryland Avenue NE, Washington, DC 20002, 202/544-6564.

United Methodist Church, General Board of Church and Society,

100 Maryland Avenue NE, Washington, DC 20002, 202/488-5600.

Commission for Racial Justice, UCC, 700 Prospect Avenue East, Cleveland, OH 44115-1100, 216/736-2168. Important study on environmental racism available.

American Baptist, USA (ABC), Valley Forge, PA 19482-0851, 215/768-2410.

Church of the Brethren, World Ministries Commission, 1451 Dundee Avenue, Elgin, IL 60120, 708/742-5100.

Episcopal Church, 815 Second Avenue, New York, NY 10017, 212/867-8400.

ELCA Division for Church and Society, 8765 Higgins Road, Chicago, IL 60641, 312/380-2708.

Presbyterian Church, USA, 100 Witherspoon St., Room 3046, Louisville, KY 40202-1396, 502/569-5809.

U.S. Catholic Conference, 3211 4th Street NE, Washington, DC 20017, 202/541-3197.

Disciples of Christ, 222 S. Downey Avenue, Indianapolis, IN 46206, 317/353-1491.

Southern Baptist Convention, 901 Commerce St., Suite 550, Nashville, TN 37203-3696, 615/244-2495.

Unitarian Universalist, Seventh Principle Project, 188 Morris Avenue, Providence, RI 02906-2405, 401/421-7362.

National Council of Churches, Eco-Justice Working Group, 475 Riverside Drive, Room 572, New York, NY 10115, 212/870-2385.

Notes

Chapter 1

1. Christopher Flavin, "Slowing Global Warming: A Worldwide Strategy," *Worldwatch Paper 91* (October 1989): 13.

2. Ibid., 29.

3. Ibid., 34–35.

4. Ibid., 57.

5. Cynthia Pollock Shea, "Protecting Life on Earth: Steps to Save the Ozone Layer," *Worldwatch Paper 87* (December 1988): 5–6.

6. Ibid., 13.

7. Ibid., 14.

8. Ibid., 15.

9. Ibid., 15–16.

10. Ibid., 17.

11. Ibid., 18.

12. Ibid., 18–27.

13. Cynthia Pollock Shea, "Protecting the Ozone Layer," in *State of the World, 1989* (New York: W. W. Norton, 1989), 80.

14. Ibid., 88.

15. Shea, *Worldwatch Paper 87*, 33.

16. Ibid., 22–23.

17. Shea, "Protecting the Ozone Layer," 93–94.

18. Shea, *Worldwatch Paper 87*, 33.

19. Ibid., 33–34.

20. Ibid., 34.

21. J. W. Maurits la Riviere, "Threats to the World's Water," *Scientific American*, September/October 1989, 80.

22. Sandra Postel, "Conserving Water: The Untapped Alternative, *Worldwatch Paper* 67 (September 1985): 14–20.

23. Ibid., 20–24.

24. Ibid., 27–34.

25. Ibid., 35.

26. "The Crisis of Water," Environmental Project on Central America (EPOCA) Green Paper No. 4.

27. H. Patricia Hynes, *Earth Right* (Rocklin, Calif.: Prima, 1990), 111–12.

28. *Arizona Trend,* January 1991.

29. *Newsweek,* November 27, 1989, 67.

30. Walter H. Corson, ed., *The Global Ecology Handbook* (Boston: Beacon, 1990), 269.

31. Cynthia Pollock, "Mining Urban Wastes: The Potential for Recycling," *Worldwatch Paper* 76 (April 1987), 22.

32. Janet Marinelli, "After the Flush: The Next Generation," *Garbage* (January/February 1990): 24–25, 35–36.

33. Flavin, "Slowing Global Warming," 37, 19, 21.

34. Ibid.

35. Ibid.

36. "Viewpoint," *BioScience* 36, no. 10 (1986): 642.

37. Sandra Postel and Lori Heise, "Reforesting the Earth," *Worldwatch Paper* 83 (April 1988): 16–17.

38. Alan B. Durning, "Ending Poverty," in *State of the World, 1990* (New York: W. W. Norton, 1990), 142.

39. Alan B. Durning, "Poverty and the Environment: Reversing the Downward Spiral," *Worldwatch Paper* 92 (November 1989): 26.

40. Jim MacNeill, "Strategies for Sustainable Economic Development," *Scientific American*, September/October 1989, 161–63.

41. World Resource Institute in collaboration with the United Nations Environmental Program and the United Nations Development Program, "Size and Growth of Population and Labor Force, 1960–2025" (Table 16.1), in *World Resources, 1990–91* (New York: Oxford University Press, 1990).

42. Lester R. Brown and John E. Young, "Feeding the World in the Nineties," in *State of the World, 1990* (New York: W. W. Norton, 1990), 66.

43. Postel and Heise, "Reforesting the Earth," 17.

44. Durning, "Ending Poverty," 139.

45. *New York Times National,* Friday, June 8, 1992.

46. Corson, *Global Ecology Handbook*, 179.

47. "Race to Save the Planet" video (Santa Barbara, Calif.), segment 8. PBS Special. For more information contact the Annenberg Collection, P.O. Box 1922, Santa Barbara, CA 93116-1922.

48. World Resources Institute et al., "Size and Growth of Population" (Table 16.1), in *World Resources, 1990–91* (New York: Oxford University Press, 1990), 254–55.

49. Brown and Young, "Feeding the World in the Nineties," 60.

50. Ibid., 61.

51. Ibid.

52. Ibid., 64.

53. Ibid., 64–65.

54. Ibid., 63.

55. Ibid., 76, 66–67.

56. D. H. Meadows et al., *Limits to Growth* (New York: Universe, 1972), 50.

57. Postel and Heise, "Reforesting the Earth," 5–8.

58. Sandra Postel, Lori Heise, and Hilary F. French, "Clearing the Air," in *State of the World, 1990* (New York: W. W. Norton, 1990), 108.

59. Postel and Heise, "Reforesting the Earth," 16–17.

60. Ibid., 19.

61. Ibid., 23.

62. Ibid., 27.

63. Ibid., 27–28.

64. Ibid., 37.

65. Ibid., 43.

66. Ibid., 47.

67. Edward C. Wolf, "On the Brink of Extinction: Preserving the Diversity of Life," *Worldwatch Paper 78* (June 1987), 5–44. Edward O. Wilson, "Threats to Biodiversity," *Scientific American*, September/October 1989, 108–16. E. O. Wilson states it this way: "As a rule of thumb, a tenfold increase in area results in a doubling of the number of species. Put the other way, if the island area is diminished tenfold, the number of species will be cut in half" (111). By island he means both a geographical island and a patch of forest surrounded by a sea of grassland.

68. Postel, Heise, and French, "Clearing the Air," 107–8.

69. Ibid., 110–11.

70. Amory Lovins, "The Soft Energy Path," in *The Center Magazine* 11, no. 5 (September–October 1978).

71. Christopher Flavin and Nicholas Lenssen, "Designing a Sustainable Energy System," in *State of the World, 1991* (New York: W. W. Norton, 1991), 23.

72. *The 1991 Information Please Almanac* (New York: Houghton Mifflin, 1990), 364.

73. Flavin and Lenssen, "Energy System," 23.

74. Ibid., 137.

75. *The World Almanac and Book of Facts* (New York: Pharos, 1990), 183.

76. *The Global 2000 Report to the President* (New York: Penguin, 1982), 172.

77. *New York Times*, August 18, 1991, business section, 1, 19.

78. William Fulkerson, Roddie R. Judkins, and Manoj K. Sanghvi, "Energy from Fossil Fuels," *Scientific American*, September 1990, 130.

79. Corson, *The Global Ecology Handbook*, 199.

80. *World Almanac*, 183.

81. Ibid.

82. *Global 2000*, 205.

83. Ibid., 212; U.S. Department of the Interior, Bureau of Mines, *Mineral Commodity Summaries* (Washington, D.C.: Government Printing Office, 1982); Corson, *Global Ecology Handbook*, 180.

84. Ibid.

85. Corson, *Global Ecology Handbook*, 179.

86. Ibid.

87. Ibid.

88. *Global 2000*, 208.

89. Ibid., 223.

Chapter 2

1. Herman E. Daly and John B. Cobb, *For the Common Good* (Boston: Beacon, 1989).

2. Theodore Roszak, *The Voice of the Earth* (New York: Simon and Schuster, 1992), 14.

3. Adam Smith, *The Theory of Moral Sentiments* (Indianapolis: Liberty Classics, 1969).

4. For more information about TOES/Americas, write to P.O. Box 12003, Austin, TX 78711.

Chapter 3

1. Robert Bellah et al., *Habits of the Heart* (Berkeley and Los Angeles: University of California Press, 1985).

2. I first met James Cone at Holden Village when he criticized me because I suggested that it is a dubious achievement to move from being a disadvantaged black to a middle-class black because the middle-class lifestyle was problematic, destructive, and an impossible goal for the rest of the world. He interpreted my statement as an ideological defense of privilege. I think that he was right to chastise me but wrong in the position he held that becoming equal with middle-class privileged persons was an adequate goal for any Christian.

3. James Cone, *For My People* (New York: Orbis, 1984), 5–6.

4. Ibid., 28.

5. Ibid., 34.

6. Ibid., 94.

7. Ibid., 150.

8. Ibid.

Select Bibliography

Global Warming

Abrahamson, Dean. *The Challenge of Global Warming.* Washington, D.C.: Island Press, 1989.

Burke, James. "After the Warming." Video. New York: Ambrose Video, 1987.

"Energy and Transportation Issues." *Scientific American,* September 1990.

Flavin, Christopher. "Slowing Global Warming." In *State of the World, 1990.* New York: W. W. Norton, 1990.

———. "Slowing Global Warming, A Worldwide Strategy." *Worldwatch Paper* 91 (October 1989).

Flavin, Christopher, and Nicholas Lenssen. "Designing a Sustainable Energy System." In *State of the World, 1991.* New York: W. W. Norton, 1991.

———. "Saving the Climate Saves Money." *Worldwatch Magazine* (November/December 1990): 26–33.

Frosch, Robert A., and Nicholas E. Galapoulos. "Strategies for Energy Use." *Scientific American,* September 1989, 136–43.

"Global Climate Change: Social and Personal Responses." *In Context* 22 (Summer 1989).

"The Greenhouse Effect: How It Can Change Our Lives." *EPA Journal* (January/February 1989).

Houghton, Richard A., and George M. Woodwell. "Global Climate Change." *Scientific American,* April 1989.

Hynes, Patricia H. "Global Warming: The Greenhouse Effect." In *Earth Right.* Rocklin, Calif.: Prima, 1990.

Legett, Jeremy, ed. "Global Warming." In *The Greenpeace Report.* New York: Oxford, 1990.

147

Lenssen, Nicholas. "Confronting Nuclear Waste." In *State of the World, 1992.* New York: W. W. Norton, 1992.

————. "Nuclear Waste, the Problem that Won't Go Away." *Worldwatch Paper* 106 (December 1991).

Lowe, Marcia D. "Alternatives to the Automobile: Transport for Livable Cities." *Worldwatch Paper* 98 (October 1990).

————. "The Bicycle: Vehicle for a Small Planet." *Worldwatch Paper* 90 (September 1989).

"The Once and Future Weather." *The Economist,* April 7, 1990.

Renner, Michael. "Rethinking the Role of the Automobile." *Worldwatch Paper* 84 (June 1988).

————. "Rethinking Transportation." In *State of the World, 1989.* New York: W. W. Norton, 1989.

Rifkin, Jeremy. *Entropy: Into the Greenhouse World.* Rev. ed. New York: Bantam, 1989.

Schneider, Stephen. "The Changing Climate." *Scientific American,* September 1989, 70–79.

————. *Global Warming.* San Francisco: Sierra Club, 1989.

————. "The Greenhouse Effect, Science and Policy." *Science* 243 (February 1989).

Smith, Joel B., and Dennis Tirpak, eds. *The Potential Effects of Global Climate Change on the United States.* Washington, D.C.: Environmental Protection Agency, 1989.

Union of Concerned Scientists. "How You Can Fight Global Warming." "The Global Warming Debate." "The Heat Is On." "Briefing Paper: Renewable Energy and Global Warming." "The Greenhouse Effect, Briefing Paper." "Motor-Vehicle Efficiency and Global Warming." Pamphlets.

Washington, Warren M. "Where's the Heat?" *Natural History,* March 1990.

Weiner, Jonathan. *The Next One Hundred Years.* New York: Bantam, 1990.

Ozone

Caplan, Ruth. "Saving Our Skins." In *Our Earth, Ourselves.* New York: Bantam, 1990, 50–75.

Gribbin, John. *The Hole in the Sky.* London: Gorgi, 1988.

Hynes, Patricia H. "The Ozone Layer: Earth's Evanescent Membrane." In *Earth Right.* Rocklin, Calif.: Prima, 1990, 135–73.

"Life under the Ozone Hole." *Newsweek,* December 9, 1991.

Lyman, Fransesca. "As the Ozone Thins, the Plot Thickens." *Amicus* (Summer 1991): 20–30.

Natural Resources Defense Council. *Saving the Ozone Layer.* Pamphlet. New York: Natural Resources Defense Council. October 1989.

Office of Technology Assessment. "Analysis of the Montreal Protocol on Substances that Deplete the Ozone Layer." In *The Challenge of Global Warming.* Ed. Dean Edwin Abrahamson. Washington, D.C.: Island Press, 1989.

Shea, Cynthia Pollock. "Mending the Earth's Shield." *World-Watch Magazine* (January/February 1989): 27–34.

———. "Protecting Life on Earth: Steps To Save the Ozone Layer." *Worldwatch Paper 87* (December 1988).

———. "Protecting the Ozone Layer." In *State of the World, 1989.* New York: W. W. Norton, 1989.

Water

Corson, Walter H., ed. "Fresh Water." In *The Global Ecology Handbook.* Boston: Beacon Press, 1990.

Hynes, H. Patricia. "Drinking Water: Toxins on Tap." In *Earth Right.* Rocklin, Calif.: Prima, 1990, 83–124.

Maurits de Riviere, J. W. "Threats to the World's Water." *Scientific American,* September 1989, 80–107.

Postel, Sandra. "Conserving Water: The Untapped Alternative." *Worldwatch Paper 67* (September 1985).

———. "Saving Water for Agriculture." In *State of the World, 1990.* New York: W. W. Norton, 1990.

———. "Trouble on Tap." *World-Watch* (September/October 1989): 12–20.

———. "Water for Agriculture: Facing the Limits." *Worldwatch Paper 93* (December 1989).

———. "Water: Rethinking Management in an Age of Scarcity." *Worldwatch Paper 62.*

Wastes

Brown, Lester, Christopher Flavin, and Sandra Postel. "Recycling and Reusing Materials." In *Saving the Planet.* New York: W. W. Norton, 1991.

Brown, Michael. "The Lower Depths: Underground Injection of Hazardous Wastes." *The Amicus Journal,* Winter 1986, 14–23.

Caplan, Ruth. "No Time to Waste." In *Our Earth, Ourselves.* New York: Bantam, 1990.

Corson, Walter H., ed. "Hazardous Substances" and "Solid Waste Management." In *The Global Ecology Handbook.* Boston: Beacon Press, 1990.

French, Hilary F. "A Most Deadly Trade." *World-Watch Magazine* (July/August 1990): 11–17.

Gilman, Robert. "The Restoration of Waters." Interview with John and Nancy Jack Todd. *In Context* (Spring 1990), 42–47.

Hynes, Patricia H. "Solid Waste: Treasure in Trash." In *Earth Right.* Rocklin, Calif.: Prima, 1990.

Lenssen, Nicholas. "Confronting Nuclear Wastes." In *State of the World, 1992*. New York: W. W. Norton, 1992.

――――. "Nuclear Waste: The Problem that Won't Go Away." *Worldwatch Paper 106* (December 1991).

Lowe, Marcia D. "Down the Tubes." *World-Watch Magazine* (March/April 1989): 22–29.

Pollock, Cynthia. "Mining Urban Wastes: The Potential for Recycling." *Worldwatch Paper 76* (April 1987).

Postel, Sandra. "Defusing the Toxic Threat: Controlling Pesticides and Industrial Wastes." *Worldwatch Paper 79* (September 1987).

Shea, Cynthia Pollock. "Building a Market for Recyclables," *World-Watch Magazine* (May/June 1988): 12–18.

UIC Energy Resource Center. *Energy Aspects of Solid Waste Management*. Chicago: University of Illinois, 1990.

Young, John E. "Reducing Waste, Saving Material." *State of the World, 1992*. New York: W. W. Norton, 1992.

Third World Economic Development

Atkisson, Alan. "The Cost of Development." Interview with Helena Norberg Hodge. *In Context 25* (Spring 1990), 28–32.

Brown, Lester R. "The Changing World Food Prospect: The Nineties and Beyond." *Worldwatch Paper 85* (October 1988).

"A Cluster of Eco-Villages." *In Context 29* (Summer 1991), 15–22.

Corson, Walter H., ed. "Development and Environment." In *The Global Ecology Handbook*. Boston: Beacon Press, 1990.

Davis, Wade. "The Penan: Community in the Rainforest." *In Context 29*, 48–51.

Durning, Alan B. "Life on the Brink." *World-Watch Magazine* (March/April 1990): 22–30.

――――. "Poverty and the Environment: Reversing the Downward Spiral." *Worldwatch Paper 92* (November 1989).

Flavin, Christopher. "Electrifying the Third World." In *State of the World, 1987*. New York: W. W. Norton, 1987.

Gilman, Robert. "Sustaining the High Plains." Interview with Chuck Schroeder. *In Context 8* (Winter 1984): 42–45.

Kennedy, Robert F., Jr. "Amazon Crude." *The Amicus Journal* (Spring 1991): 24–32.

Reddy, Amulya K. N., and Jose Goldember. "Energy for the Developing World." *Scientific American*, September 1990, 110–19.

Ridgeway, James. "Micronesia, America's Third World," *The Amicus Journal* (Fall 1983).

Train, Russell E. "Sustainability, Conservation, and Development in the Third World." *The Amicus Journal* (Fall 1983).

Wagmari, Maathai. "You Strike the Woman." In Context 28 (Spring 1991), 55–57.
Wolf, Edward C. "Beyond the Green Revolution: Approaches for Third World Agriculture." Worldwatch Paper 73 (October 1986).

Population Explosion

Brown, Lester R. "Analyzing the Demographic Trap." State of the World, 1987. New York: W. W. Norton, 1987.
———. "Feeding Six Billion." World-Watch Magazine (September/October, 1989): 32–41.
Brown, Lester R., Christopher Flavin, and Sandra Postel. "A Stable World Population." In Saving the Planet. New York: W. W. Norton, 1991.
Ehrlich, Paul R., and Anne H. Ehrlich. "Population and Development Misunderstood." The Amicus Journal (Summer 1986): 8–10.
———. "The Population Explosion." The Amicus Journal (Winter 1990): 22–29.
———. The Population Explosion. New York: Simon and Schuster, 1990.
Jacobson, Jodi. "Improving Women's Reproductive Health." In State of the World, 1992. New York: W. W. Norton, 1992.
———. "India's Misconceived Family Plan." World-Watch Magazine (November/December, 1991): 18–25.
Keyfitz, Nathan. "The Growing Human Population." Scientific American, September 1989, 118–27.

Soil and Croplands

Brown, Lester R. "Breakthrough on Soil." World-Watch Magazine (May/June 1988): 19–25.
———. "Sustaining World Agriculture." In State of the World, 1987. New York: W. W. Norton, 1987.
Brown, Lester R., and Edward C. Wolf. "Soil Erosion: Quiet Crisis in the World." Worldwatch Paper 60 (September 1984).
Durning, Alan. "Fat of the Land." World-Watch Magazine (May/June 1991): 11–17.
Jacobson, Jodi. "Abandoning Homelands." State of the World, 1989. New York: W. W. Norton, 1989.
Postel, Sandra. "Halting Land Degradation." In State of the World, 1989. New York: W. W. Norton, 1989.

Forests

Atkisson, Alan. "Living Restoration." In Context 22 (Summer 1989), 48–53.
Corson, Walter H., ed. "Tropical Forests." In The Global Ecology Handbook. Boston: Beacon Press, 1990.

Flynn, John. "Timber's Last Stand." *World-Watch Magazine* (July/August 1990): 27–34.

Postel, Sandra. "Air Pollution, Acid Rain, and the Future of Forests." *World-Watch Magazine* 58 (March 1984).

———. "Reforming Forestry." *State of the World, 1991.* New York: W. W. Norton, 1991.

Postel, Sandra, and Lóri Heise. "Reforesting the Earth." *Worldwatch Paper 83* (April 1988).

Schiff, Stenley D. "The Pine Barrens." *Amicus* 7 (Spring 1986).

Waldsterben, Don Henrichsen. "Forest Death Syndrome." *Amicus* 7 (Spring 1986).

Loss of Species

Brown, Lester R., Christopher Flavin, and Sandra Postel. "Protecting the Biological Base." In *Saving the Planet.* New York: W. W. Norton, 1991.

Corson, Walter H., ed. "Biological Diversity." In *The Global Ecology Handbook.* Boston: Beacon Press, 1990.

Ryan, John C. "Conserving Biological Diversity." *State of the World, 1992.* New York: W. W. Norton, 1992.

Wilson, Edward O. "Threats to Biodiversity." *Scientific American,* September 1989, 108–17.

Wolf, Edward C. "On the Brink of Extinction: Conserving the Diversity of Life." *Worldwatch Paper 78* (June 1987).

Clean Air

Anderson, Frederick R., Daniel R. Mandelker, and A. Dan Tarlock. *Environmental Protection.* Boston: Little, Brown, 1990.

Corson, Walter H., ed. "Air, Atmosphere, and Climate." In *The Global Ecology Handbook.* Boston: Beacon Press, 1990.

Environmental Law Statues. St. Paul: West, 1991

French, Hilary F. "Clearing the Air." In *State of the World, 1990.* New York: W. W. Norton, 1990.

———. "Clearing the Air." *Worldwatch Paper 94* (January 1990).

Postel, Sandra. "Air Pollution, Acid Rain, and the Future of Forests." *Worldwatch Paper 58* (March 1984).

Minerals—Fuels and Nonfuels

Corson, Walter H., ed. "Nonfuel Minerals." In *The Global Ecology Handbook.* Boston: Beacon Press, 1990.

World Resources Institute in collaboration with the United Nations Environmental Program and the United Nations Development Program. *World Resources 1990–91.* New York: Oxford, 1990.

Young, John E. "Mining the Earth." *State of the World, 1992.* New York: W. W. Norton, 1992.

Economic Theory and Practice

Berry, Thomas. *Dream of the Earth.* San Francisco: Sierra Club, 1988.

Clark, Richard. "The Economy of Addiction." *Human Economy* (December 1988).

Clark, William. "Visions of a Sustainable Society." *The Egg* (Summer 1990).

Daly, Herman, and John Cobb. *For the Common Good.* Boston: Beacon Press, 1989.

Green Forum, Philippines. *An Alternative Development Economics.* Manila: Popular Book Store, 1991.

Henderson, Hazel. "Economics in the Solar Age." *In Context* (Spring 1990).

Heyne, Paul. *The Economic Way of Thinking.* 6th ed. Chicago: Science Research Associates, 1991.

Lowry, Susan Meeker. *Economics as if the Earth Really Mattered.* Philadelphia: New Society Publishers, 1988.

Meeks, Douglas. *God the Economist.* Philadelphia: Fortress-Augsburg, 1989.

Mollner, Terry. "The Third Way Is Here." *In Context* 19 (Autumn 1988).

Postel, Sandra. "Toward a New 'Eco Nomics.'" *World-Watch Magazine* (September/October 1990).

Waring, Marilyn. "Measuring the Economy: People, Pollution, and Politics." *Building Economic Alternatives* (Fall 1990).

———. *If Women Counted: A New Feminist Economics.* San Francisco: Harper and Row, 1988.

Education

Berry, Thomas. "The American College in the Ecological Age." In *The Dream of the Earth.* San Francisco: Sierra Club, 1990.

Blau, Sheridan D., and John von B. Rodenbeck. "Education for Survival: Toward a Human Future." In *The House We Live In.* New York: Macmillan, 1971, 483–515.

Daly, Herman, and John Cobb. "Economics as an Academic Discipline." In *For the Common Good.* Boston: Beacon Press, 1989.

"Educational Models: Four Programs." In *Cry of the Environment,* edited by Philip N. Joranson and Ken Butigan. Santa Fe: Bear, 1984.

Politics

Bahro, Rudolph. *Building the Green Movement.* Philadelphia: New Society, 1986.

Blau, Sheridan D., and John von B. Rodenbeck. "Human Institutions: Economics and Politics." In *The House We Live In.* New York: MacMillan, 1971, 439–81.

During, Alan B. "Mobilizing the Grassroots." In *State of the World, 1989.* New York: W. W. Norton, 1989.

Gore, Al. *Earth in the Balance.* Boston: Houghton Mifflin, 1992.

"Making It Happen, Effective Strategies for Changing the World." *In Context* 28 (Spring 1991).

Waring, Marilyn. *If Women Counted: A New Feminist Economics.* San Francisco: Harper and Row, 1988.

Theology

Berry, Thomas. *Dream of the Earth.* San Francisco: Sierra Club, 1990.

Birch, C., and John Cobb. *Liberation of Life.* Cambridge, England: Cambridge University Press, 1981.

Committee of Social Witness, Presbyterian Church (USA). *Restoring Creation: For Ecology and Justice.* Louisville: Office of the General Assembly, Presbyterian Church U.S.A. 1990.

Cone, James. *For My People.* New York: Orbis, 1984.

Daly, Herman E., and John Cobb. *For the Common Good.* Boston: Beacon Press 1989.

Eisler, Riane. *The Chalice and the Blade.* Cambridge, Mass.: Harper and Row, 1987.

Hall, Douglas John. *Imaging God: Dominion as Stewardship.* Grand Rapids: Eerdmans and Friendship Press, 1986.

Moltmann, Jürgen. *God in Creation.* London: SCM Press, 1985.

Soelle, Dorothy, and Shirley A. Cloyes. *To Work and To Care: A Theology of Creation.* Philadelphia: Fortress, 1984.

Index

28–29; explosion, 24–29; and forests, 21–22; growth by country, 25; in Mexico, 27
Poverty, 26
Praxis, 88–89

Recycling, 17, 111–12, 124–25
Resource depletion, 2, 29–34
Responses to Word of God: regarding carbon dioxide emissions, 111–13; regarding developing world economy, 114–15; regarding economic theory and practice, 116–18; regarding global citizenship, 119–20; in the natural world, 111–20; regarding ozone depletion, 115–16; regarding population explosion, 118–19; regarding wastes, 113–14; regarding water, 116
Riverside Church, 100, 132–37
Romans 1:18–20, 70–71
Roszak, Theodore, 59

Self-initiation, 47–49, 60, 64, 67
Socialism, 62, 84
Soil depletion, 30–31
Species depletion, 2, 34

State of the World, 97, 102

Ten ecological commandments, 101–2
Thrice-born Christian, 95
Tillich, Paul, 75–78, 82–84
Trees, 6, 34

University Church Ecological Inventory, 129–31
UV-B, 8

Values, viii, 43–44, 54, 56, 58

Wastes, 2; citizen action regarding, 111–13; organic treatment of, 18–19; water treatment of, 12–13, 15–19
Water, 1, 10–15; agricultural, 12; in Arizona, 14; citizen action regarding, 116; conservation of, 12; in El Salvador, 12; pollution, 14; quality, 12; recycling, 12
Whitehead, Alfred North, 67, 75
Wieman, Henry Nelson, 75
Wood: fuel, 21–22, 31–32; industrial, 32–33
Word of God, ix, 3, 69–75, 87–89, 90–111